AN ECONOMIC THEORIST'S BOOK OF TALES

An economic theorist's book of tales

Essays that entertain the consequences of new assumptions
in economic theory

GEORGE A. AKERLOF

University of California, Berkeley

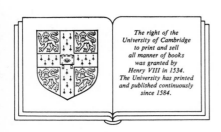

The right of the
University of Cambridge
to print and sell
all manner of books
was granted by
Henry VIII in 1534.
The University has printed
and published continuously
since 1584.

CAMBRIDGE UNIVERSITY PRESS

CAMBRIDGE

LONDON   NEW YORK   NEW ROCHELLE

MELBOURNE   SYDNEY

Published by the Press Syndicate of the University of Cambridge
The Pitt Building, Trumpington Street, Cambridge CB2 1RP
32 East 57th Street, New York, N.Y. 10022, USA
296 Beaconsfield Parade, Middle Park, Melbourne 3206, Australia

First published 1984

Printed in the United States of America

Library of Congress Cataloging in Publication Data
Akerlof, George A., 1940–
An economic theorist's book of tales.
Includes index.
1. Economics – Addresses, essays, lectures.
2. Economics – Methodology – Addresses, essays, lectures.
I. Title.
HB71.A34   1984   330.1   84–3225
ISBN 0 521 26323 9 hard covers
ISBN 0 521 26933 4 paperback

Contents

Acknowledgments

I would like to single out four persons who have been especially helpful in writing these essays. Of course, many others have made comments and criticisms. They are thanked (many of them many times) in the individual essays. This special space I would like to reserve for these people, who not only have helped with specific essays but also contributed generally to my education.

First, I would like to thank Robert Solow. Each of the models in this volume is a short statement that focuses on a problem. This method of economic theory was taught by Solow to a generation of graduate students at MIT via the medium of growth models. Through his students his influence has gone far beyond his own original contributions. I am proud to be one of these students.

"The Market for 'Lemons'" was written in my first year at Berkeley, 1966–67. It might not have been written without the encouragement of Thomas Rothenberg. And it might not have been published without his constructive criticisms, especially in phrasing the proofs in terms of supply and demand. His help went far beyond that expected of a colleague, or even a good friend.

Michael Rothschild was the editor of the symposium that published "The Economics of Caste and of the Rat Race and Other Woeful Tales." He gave me great trouble. He did not like the early versions. He made painstaking comments, and the paper improved. I learned a lot from him about how to write an essay of the sort published in this volume. His teachings went beyond the specific help on the specific essay.

Finally, in this special list, Janet Yellen has listened to my problems for the last six years. The last five essays here were all written under her influence. She has encouraged my writing and also dissuaded me from working on things that would have been mistakes. For personal reasons, far in addition to her invaluable helpfulness with this work, I would like to dedicate this book to her.

The author and the Cambridge University Press wish to thank the publishers of the following essays for permission to reprint them in this volume.

Chapter 2. "The Market for 'Lemons': Quality Uncertainty and the Market Mechanism," *The Quarterly Journal of Economics, 84,* August 1970, 488–500. Reprinted by permission of John Wiley & Sons, Inc. Copyright 1970 by the President and Fellows of Harvard College.

Chapter 3. "The Economics of Caste and of the Rat Race and Other Woeful Tales," *The Quarterly Journal of Economics, 90,* November 1976, 599–617. Reprinted by permission of John Wiley & Sons, Inc. Copyright 1976 by the President and Fellows of Harvard College.

Chapter 4. "The Economics of 'Tagging' as Applied to the Optimal Income Tax, Welfare Programs, and Manpower Planning," *American Economic Review, 68,* March 1978, 8–19. Reprinted by permission of the American Economic Association. Copyright 1978 by the American Economic Association.

Chapter 5. "A Theory of Social Custom, of Which Unemployment May Be One Consequence," *The Quarterly Journal of Economics, 94,* June 1980, 749–75. Reprinted by permission of John Wiley & Sons, Inc. Copyright 1980 by the President and Fellows of Harvard College.

Chapter 6. "Jobs as Dam Sites," *The Review of Economic Studies, 48,* January 1981, 37–49. Reprinted by permission of *The Review of Economic Studies.* Copyright 1981 by *The Review of Economic Studies.*

Chapter 7. "The Economic Consequences of Cognitive Dissonance," *American Economic Review, 72,* June 1982, 307–19. Reprinted by permission of the American Economic Association. Copyright 1982 by the American Economic Association.

Chapter 8. "Labor Contracts as Partial Gift Exchange," *The Quarterly Journal of Economics, 97,* November 1982, 543–69. Reprinted by permission of John Wiley & Sons, Inc. Copyright 1982 by the President and Fellows of Harvard College.

Chapter 9. "Loyalty Filters," *American Economic Review, 73,* March 1983, 54–63. Reprinted by permission of the American Economic Association. Copyright 1983 by the American Economic Association.

1

Introduction

This book is a collection of previously published essays. It makes sense as a collection because these essays have more to say together than the sum of each individually. That collective message is largely methodological. It concerns the possibility of a style of economic theory rather different from the current stock in most economic journals.

What mainly differentiates these articles from most economic theory today is their willingness to entertain the consequences of new assumptions. Most of the best economic theory of the last forty years has concerned the consequences of application of supply and demand theory to new areas (such as resource economics, the demand and supply of patents, the economics of discrimination, and the economics of foreign exchange markets) and also to the solution of classical problems (such as proof of the existence of equilibrium and the Pareto optimality of that equilibrium in a classical Walrasian model).

In contrast, these essays represent an alternative approach to the advance of economic theory. That alternative approach is to explore the consequences of new behavioral assumptions. To give one example of this exploration, prior to the publication of "The Market for 'Lemons'" there was very little work on the economic consequences of imperfect information (except in formal game theory). This omission is curious because information imperfections are consistent with economists' utilitarian view of the world. Since the early 1970s, however, a large literature has grown up on the consequences of imperfect information, some of it concerned with the topic of "asymmetric information," the concept explored in that paper. The innovation of that paper, as much as any specific results presented there, was the introduction of that concept into economic theory.

Economic theory is written according to a set of traditional rules. Typically, economic theorists – or at least the *neoclassical* theorists who dominate our profession today – are concerned with market equilibria in which individual actors behave selfishly and usually with expectations that, if not precisely correct, nevertheless make

1

sense in terms of the individuals' respective environments. These expectations are in this sense rational, either in the technical or non-technical sense of that word. Prior to 1970 this theory was written mostly with perfect information; now that tradition has changed.

These strict, although unwritten, rules underlying economic theory allow results to be assessed and compared. For example, it is immediately clear, given the restriction of models that economists usually consider, that proof of existence of equilibrium and its Pareto optimality in the Arrow-Debreu model is canonical. Somehow this result is useful for analyzing the whole class of models considered by economic theory.

The unwritten rules that only *economic phenomena* be considered in economic models, with agents as individualistic, selfish maximizers, restrict the range of economic theory and in some cases even cause the economics profession to appear peculiarly absurd – because, without relaxation of these rules, certain *almost indisputable* economic facts, such as the existence of involuntary unemployment, become inconsistent with economic theory. Such is the case in the so-called rational expectations models of macroeconomics. These models are inconsistent with persistent high unemployment rates, as occur over the course of a business cycle, mainly because these models rely on market clearing. (Or, to be more careful, such models cannot *convincingly* explain persistent high unemployment, since with suitable torture of parameters such persistence can be shown to occur.)

My view of economic theory differs from that of most economic theorists. Most theorists, I believe, would say that good economic theory concerns interesting outcomes in models in which all agents engage in individualistic maximizing behavior. Individualistic maximizing behavior constitutes an assumption that sharply restricts the domain of possible economic models. It is an assumption that turns out to be surprisingly restrictive. It thus limits the number of possible economic models and allows easy assessment of the *interest* of any particular result.

Alternatively phrased, the preceding argument could be summarized by saying that economic theorists, like French chefs in regard to food, have developed stylized models whose ingredients are limited by some unwritten rules. Just as traditional French cooking does not use seaweed or raw fish, so neoclassical models do not make assumptions derived from psychology, anthropology, or sociology. I disagree with any rules that limit the nature of the ingredients in economic models.

In contrast to the unwritten rules whereby only certain stylized models are considered good economic theory, my own definition of "good economic theory" is that it poses interesting "if . . . then . . ." propositions relevant to some economic issue. As an example from classical economics, such a proposition would be the existence of a Pareto-optimal general equilibrium (the *then* statement) *if* the assumptions of the Arrow-Debreu model are satisfied.

There are two significant parts to this definition: one is the adjective *interesting,* the other is the phrase *relevant to some economic issue.* What constitutes an economic issue is empirically defined. According to Samuelson, interesting economic issues concern the *what, how,* and *for whom* of the distribution and use of economic resources. Macroeconomists, to give another example, tend to worry about such things as unemployment, inflation, and productivity growth as their "final" concerns, but they also worry about such things as interest rates, exchange rates, investment, consumption, taxes, and deficits as intermediate concerns. Propositions explaining all these variables may concern an *economic issue.*

A second requirement for an *interesting* propositional (i.e., if . . . then . . .) statement is some surprise relative to what is implicit (or perhaps explicit) in the usual economics literature. Thus my definition of good economic theory says that such theory must take into account economic realities (which define the variables of interest) on the one hand, and economic theory, on the other hand. In this latter regard it is necessary to refer back to existing economic theory to know what will constitute a surprise.

Indeed, the very absence of psychological, anthropological, and sociological factors in economic theory allows a whole new field of potential interest today. (Just as the absence of informational considerations allowed an untapped field for economic theory whose first explorations began about fifteen years ago.) The very absence of these psychological-anthropological-sociological behaviors allows the economic theorist to ask what the consequences of these behaviors will be for the usual economic results, derived either on the assumption that these factors can be trivially incorporated into the usual model or else on the assumption that these factors can be totally ignored. In what way will the introduction of these factors alter the traditional equilibria? Will such factors explain unemployment? Will such factors lead to interesting deviations from Pareto-optimal equilibria? Will such factors explain the nature of discrimination in a way deeper than blaming it on "tastes"? Perhaps these tastes will be endogenously explained and there can be interesting equilibria. Perhaps the introduction of these factors will yield economic models of caste and class.

One formulation of the basic idea of economic theory is exploration of the implications of equilibria in which no individuals can by any form of arbitrage make *very large* profits. In all of these chapters this basic idea underlies the notion of equilibrium. But within this conventional framework of equilibrium these essays explore nonconventional assumptions. Examples are asymmetric information, caste behavior, obedience to social customs motivated by the anthropological literature on culture, the nature of jobs, the obedience to work norms as motivated by the sociological literature, behavior according to cognitive dissonance, and the acquisition of loyalty (and personality traits).

The discussions in this volume as they now appear deal with many economic issues but, in honesty, it should be confessed that all are the direct or indirect result of a personal agenda, which is nowhere stated. My father periodically lost his job and the possibility of long-term unemployment (although it never actually occurred) was both sufficiently real and sufficiently frightening that solution of problems of unemployment became an emotional as well as an intellectual goal. My hidden agenda has always been to contribute to the solution of problems of unemployment.

Recently, solution of the problem of discrimination has been added to this agenda. This is, of course, a goal worthy for its own sake. But, also, discrimination, along with unemployment, is one of the few major economic phenomena for which market-clearing models of demand and supply offer insufficient explanation. Quite conceivably, correct models of involuntary unemployment and models of discrimination are sufficiently close that they constitute the study of the same formal phenomenon.

The first two chapters, "The Market for 'Lemons'" and "The Economics of Caste and of the Rat Race," were initially begun as attempts to think about forms of contract that would cause cyclical economic behavior, including involuntary unemployment. Deficiencies of attempts to explain unemployment by imperfect information from such an approach have been the impetus for the three chapters that are explicitly about unemployment: "A Theory of Social Custom, of Which Unemployment May Be One Consequence," "Jobs as Dam Sites," and "Labor Contracts as Partial Gift Exchange." These chapters rely on almost perfect information because three problems are always present in models of unemployment which rely on imperfect information. First, people with the lowest training costs and whose output is easiest to measure – low-educated, unskilled workers – always have the highest unemployment rates. If imperfect information coupled with high training costs is the chief reason for involuntary unemployment, on the contrary, managerial employees, with high training costs and output that is difficult to gauge, should have almost the highest unemployment rates. Second, the loss from misestimating labor quality in a *perfect* market is low, since in such a market workers can be dismissed as soon as it is discovered that their wages are higher than the market rate for labor of that quality. Third, it is often surprising how truthful sellers are to buyers who ask the right questions, so that imperfect *asymmetric* information may be a less potent phenomenon than is suggested by a world view that sees all people as selfish maximizers. As Max Weber has sharply pointed out: Benjamin Franklin, in urging the utilitarian reasons for truthfulness, is himself more truthful than consistent with his own dicta.

Consistent with its title, this book is the economic theorist's equivalent of a collection of short stories by a single author. What such short stories usually have in common is a style and some common ideas. Here the common ideas are the application of asymmetric information problems in Chapters 2, 3, and 4 and the application of concepts from anthropology, psychology, and sociology in the last five chapters. All eight have in common, as already stated, the "use" of new ingredients in economic theory.

Exploration of the consequences of imperfect information for economic theory needs no plea for further work since imperfect information is now a standard consideration of economic theorists. However, economists have ignored the other social sciences and continue to do so. At its worst, such ignorance may have deprived economists of a sensible theory of unemployment and probably also of a good theory of discrimination. So the lack of consideration of the findings of the other social sciences may make differences of practical importance.

I would like to think that psycho- socio- anthropo-economics is at the beginning of a period when many people will be working in this area. Thirty years ago mathematical economics was probably at a similar stage of development. It is the purpose of this volume to demonstrate that a certain style of paper can be systematically written (otherwise how could there be *eight* of them?). Nevertheless, this field has not reached the stage where there is a set of problems with a natural research agenda. That will be necessary, however, before this area becomes a "field" like mathematical economics today. Could such a field develop with a similar collection of scholars working on the applications of other social sciences to economics? It is the purpose of this collection to demonstrate that such work is possible.

2

The market for "lemons": quality uncertainty and the market mechanism

I. Introduction

This paper relates quality and uncertainty. The existence of goods of many grades poses interesting and important problems for the theory of markets. On the one hand, the interaction of quality differences and uncertainty may explain important institutions of the labor market. On the other hand, this paper presents a struggling attempt to give structure to the statement: "Business in underdeveloped countries is difficult"; in particular, a structure is given for determining the economic costs of dishonesty. Additional applications of the theory include comments on the structure of money markets, on the notion of "insurability," on the liquidity of durables, and on brand-name goods.

There are many markets in which buyers use some market statistic to judge the quality of prospective purchases. In this case there is incentive for sellers to market poor quality merchandise, since the returns for good quality accrue mainly to the entire group whose statistic is affected rather than to the individual seller. As a result there tends to be a reduction in the average quality of goods and also in the size of the market. It should also be perceived that in these markets social and private returns differ, and therefore, in some cases, governmental intervention may increase the welfare of all parties. Or private institutions may arise to take advantage of the potential increases in welfare which can accrue to all parties. By nature, however, these institutions are nonatomistic, and therefore concentrations of power – with ill consequences of their own – can develop.

The automobile market is used as a finger exercise to illustrate and

The author would especially like to thank Thomas Rothenberg for invaluable comments and inspiration. In addition he is indebted to Roy Radner, Albert Fishlow, Bernard Saffran, William D. Nordhaus, Giorgio La Malfa, Charles C. Holt, John Letiche, and the referee for help and suggestions. He would also like to thank the Indian Statistical Institute and the Ford Foundation for financial support.

develop these thoughts. It should be emphasized that this market is chosen for its concreteness and ease in understanding rather than for its importance or realism.

II. The model with automobiles as an example

A. The automobiles market

The example of used cars captures the essence of the problem. From time to time one hears either mention of or surprise at the large price difference between new cars and those which have just left the show-room. The usual lunch table justification for this phenomenon is the pure joy of owning a "new" car. We offer a different explanation. Suppose (for the sake of clarity rather than reality) that there are just four kinds of cars. There are new cars and used cars. There are good cars and bad cars (which in America are known as "lemons"). A new car may be a good car or a lemon, and of course the same is true of used cars.

The individuals in this market buy a new automobile without knowing whether the car they buy will be good or a lemon. But they do know that with probability q it is a good car and with probability $(1 - q)$ it is a lemon; by assumption, q is the proportion of good cars produced and $(1 - q)$ is the proportion of lemons.

After owning a specific car, however, for a length of time, the car owner can form a good idea of the quality of this machine; i.e., the owner assigns a new probability to the event that his car is a lemon. This estimate is more accurate than the original estimate. An asymmetry in available information has developed, for the sellers now have more knowledge about the quality of a car than the buyers. But good cars and bad cars must still sell at the same price – since it is impossible for a buyer to tell the difference between a good car and a bad car. It is apparent that a used car cannot have the same valuation as a new car – if it did have the same valuation, it would clearly be advantageous to trade a lemon at the price of a new car, and buy another new car, at a higher probability q of being good and a lower probability of being bad. Thus the owner of a good machine must be locked in. Not only is it true that he cannot receive the true value of his car, but he cannot even obtain the expected value of a new car.

Gresham's law has made a modified reappearance. For most cars traded will be the "lemons," and good cars may not be traded at all. The "bad" cars tend to drive out the good (in much the same way that bad money drives out the good). But the analogy with Gresham's law is not quite complete: bad cars drive out the good because they sell at the same price as good cars; similarly, bad money drives out good because the exchange rate is even. But the bad cars sell at the same price as good cars since it is impossible for a buyer to tell the difference between a good and a bad car; only the seller knows. In Gresham's law, however, presumably both buyer and seller can tell the difference between good and bad money. So the analogy is instructive, but not complete.

B. Asymmetrical information

It has been seen that the good cars may be driven out of the market by the lemons. But in a more continuous case with different grades of goods, even worse pathologies can exist. For it is quite possible to have the bad driving out the not-so-bad driving out the medium driving out the not-so-good driving out the good in such a sequence of events that no market exists at all.

One can assume that the demand for used automobiles depends most strongly upon two variables – the price of the automobile p and the average quality of used cars traded, μ, or $Q^d = D(p, \mu)$. Both the supply of used cars and also the average quality μ will depend upon the price, or $\mu = \mu(p)$ and $S = S(p)$. And in equilibrium the supply must equal the demand for the given average quality, or $S(p) = D(p, \mu(p))$. As the price falls, normally the quality will also fall. And it is quite possible that no goods will be traded at any price level.

Such an example can be derived from utility theory. Assume that there are just two groups of traders: groups one and two. Give group one a utility function

$$U_1 = M + \sum_{i=1}^{n} x_i$$

where M is the consumption of goods other than automobiles, x_i is the quality of the ith automobile, and n is the number of automobiles.

Similarly, let

$$U_2 = M + \sum_{i=1}^{n} \tfrac{3}{2} x_i$$

where M, x_i, and n are defined as before.

Three comments should be made about these utility functions: (1) Without linear utility (say with logarithmic utility) one gets needlessly mired in algebraic complication. (2) The use of linear utility allows a focus on the effects of asymmetry of information; with a concave utility function we would have to deal jointly with the usual risk-variance effects of uncertainty and the special effects we wish to discuss here. (3) U_1 and U_2 have the odd characteristic that the addition of a second car, or indeed a kth car, adds the same amount of utility as the first. Again realism is sacrificed to avoid a diversion from the proper focus.

To continue, it is assumed (1) that both type one traders and type two traders are von Neumann-Morgenstern maximizers of expected utility; (2) that group one has N cars with uniformly distributed quality x, $0 \leq x \leq 2$, and group two has no cars; (3) that the price of "other goods" M is unity.

Denote the income (including that derived from the sale of automobiles) of all type one traders as Y_1 and the income of all type two traders as Y_2. The demand for used cars will be the sum of the demands by both groups. When one ignores indivisibilities, the demand for automobiles by type one traders will be

$$D_1 = Y_1/p \qquad \mu/p > 1$$
$$D_1 = 0 \qquad \mu/p < 1.$$

And the supply of cars offered by type one traders is

(1) $S_1 = pN/2 \qquad p \leq 2$

with average quality

(2) $\mu = p/2.$

(To derive (1) and (2), the uniform distribution of automobile quality is used.)

Similarly the demand of type two traders is

$$D_2 = Y_2/p \qquad 3\mu/2 > p$$
$$D_2 = 0 \qquad 3\mu/2 < p$$

and

$$S_2 = 0.$$

Thus total demand $D(p, \mu)$ is

$$D(p, \mu) = (Y_2 + Y_1)/p \qquad \text{if } p < \mu$$
$$D(p, \mu) = Y_2/p \qquad \text{if } \mu < p < 3\mu/2$$
$$D(p, \mu) = 0 \qquad \text{if } p > 3\mu/2.$$

However, with price p, average quality is $p/2$ and therefore at no price will any trade take place at all, in spite of the fact that *at any given price* between 0 and 3 there are traders of type one who are willing to sell their automobiles at a price which traders of type two are willing to pay.

C. Symmetric information

The foregoing is contrasted with the case of symmetric information. Suppose that the quality of all cars is uniformly distributed, $0 \leq x \leq 2$. Then the demand curves and supply curves can be written as follows:

Supply

$$S(p) = N \qquad p > 1$$
$$S(p) = 0 \qquad p < 1.$$

And the demand curves are

$$D(p) = (Y_2 + Y_1)/p \qquad p < 1$$
$$D(p) = (Y_2/p) \qquad 1 < p < \frac{3}{2}$$
$$D(p) = 0 \qquad p > \frac{3}{2}.$$

In equilibrium

(3) $p = 1$ if $Y_2 < N$
(4) $p = Y_2/N$ if $2Y_2/3 < N < Y_2$
(5) $p = \frac{3}{2}$ if $N < 2Y_2/3$.

If $N < Y_2$ there is a gain in utility over the case of asymmetrical information of $N/2$. (If $N > Y_2$, in which case the income of type two traders is insufficient to buy all N automobiles, there is a gain in utility of $Y_2/2$ units.)

Finally, it should be mentioned that in this example, if traders of groups one and two have the same probabilistic estimates about the quality of individual automobiles – though these estimates may vary from automobile to automobile – (3), (4), and (5) will still describe equilibrium with one slight change: p will then represent the expected price of one quality unit.

III. Examples and applications

A. Insurance

It is a well-known fact that people over 65 have great difficulty in buying medical insurance. The natural question arises: why doesn't the price rise to match the risk?

Our answer is that as the price level rises the people who insure themselves will be those who are increasingly certain that they will need the insurance, for error in medical check-ups, doctors' sympathy with older patients, and so on make it much easier for the applicant to assess the risks involved than the insurance company. The result is that the average medical condition of insurance applicants deteri-orates as the price level rises – with the result that no insurance sales may take place at any price.[1] This is strictly analogous to our automobiles case, where the average quality of used cars supplied fell

1 Arrow's fine article, "Uncertainty and Medical Care" (*American Economic Review,* Vol. 53, 1963), does not make this point explicitly. He emphasizes "moral hazard" rather than "adverse selection." In its strict sense, the presence of "moral hazard" is equally disadvantageous for both governmental and private programs; in its broader sense, which includes "adverse selection," "moral hazard" gives a decided advantage to government insurance programs.

with a corresponding fall in the price level. This agrees with the explanation in insurance textbooks:

> Generally speaking policies are not available at ages materially greater than sixty-five. . . . The term premiums are too high for any but the most pessimistic (which is to say the least healthy) insureds to find attractive. Thus there is a severe problem of adverse selection at these ages.[2]

The statistics do not contradict this conclusion. While demands for health insurance rise with age, a 1956 national sample survey of 2,809 families with 8,898 persons shows that hospital insurance coverage drops from 63 per cent of those aged 45 to 54, to 31 per cent for those over 65. And surprisingly, this survey also finds average medical expenses for males aged 55 to 64 of $88, while males over 65 pay an average of $77.[3] While noninsured expenditure rises from $66 to $80 in these age groups, insured expenditure declines from $105 to $70. The conclusion is tempting that insurance companies are particularly wary of giving medical insurance to older people.

The principle of "adverse selection" is potentially present in all lines of insurance. The following statement appears in an insurance textbook written at the Wharton School:

> There is potential adverse selection in the fact that healthy term insurance policy holders may decide to terminate their coverage when they become older and premiums mount. This action could leave an insurer with an undue proportion of below average risks and claims might be higher than anticipated. Adverse selection "appears (or at least is possible) whenever the individual or group insured has freedom to buy or not to buy, to choose the amount or plan of insurance, and to persist or to discontinue as a policy holder."[4]

Group insurance, which is the most common form of medical insurance in the United States, picks out the healthy, for generally

2 O. D. Dickerson, *Health Insurance* (Homewood, Ill.: Irwin, 1959), p. 333.
3 O. W. Anderson (with J. J. Feldman), *Family Medical Costs and Insurance* (New York: McGraw-Hill, 1956).
4 H. S. Denenberg, R. D. Eilers, G. W. Hoffman, C. A. Kline, J. J. Melone, and H. W. Snider, *Risk and Insurance* (Englewood Cliffs, N.J.: Prentice Hall, 1964), p. 446.

adequate health is a precondition for employment. At the same time this means that medical insurance is least available to those who need it most, for the insurance companies do their own "adverse selection."

This adds one major argument in favor of Medicare.[5] On a cost-benefit basis Medicare may pay off, for it is quite possible that every individual in the market would be willing to pay the expected cost of his Medicare and buy insurance, yet no insurance company can afford to sell him a policy – for at any price it will attract too many "lemons." The welfare economics of Medicare, in this view, is *exactly* analogous to the usual classroom argument for public expenditure on roads.

B. The employment of minorities

The Lemons Principle also casts light on the employment of minorities. Employers may refuse to hire members of minority groups for certain types of jobs. This decision may not reflect irrationality or prejudice – but profit maximization. For race may serve as a good *statistic* for the applicant's social background, quality of schooling, and general job capabilities.

Good quality schooling could serve as a substitute for this statistic; by grading students the schooling system can give a better indicator of quality than other more superficial characteristics. As T. W. Schultz writes, "The educational establishment *discovers* and cultivates potential talent. The capabilities of children and mature students can never be known until *found* and cultivated."[6] (Italics added.) An untrained worker may have valuable natural talents, but these talents must be certified by "the educational establishment"

---

5 The following quote, again taken from an insurance textbook, shows how far the medical insurance market is from perfect competition:

> " . . . insurance companies must screen their applicants. Naturally it is true that many people will voluntarily seek adequate insurance on their own initiative. But in such lines as accident and health insurance, companies are likely to give a second look to persons who voluntarily seek insurance without being approached by an agent." (F. J. Angell, *Insurance, Principles and Practices*, New York: The Ronald Press, 1957, pp. 8–9.)

This shows that insurance is *not* a commodity for sale on the open market.

6 T. W. Schultz, *The Economic Value of Education* (New York: Columbia University Press, 1964), p. 42.

before a company can afford to use them. The certifying establishment, however, must be credible; the unreliability of slum schools decreases the economic possibilities of their students.

This lack may be particularly disadvantageous to members of already disadvantaged minority groups. For an employer may make a rational decision not to hire any members of these groups in responsible positions – because it is difficult to distinguish those with good job qualifications from those with bad qualifications. This type of decision is clearly what George Stigler had in mind when he wrote, "in a regime of ignorance Enrico Fermi would have been a gardener, von Neumann a checkout clerk at a drugstore."[7]

As a result, however, the rewards for work in slum schools tend to accrue to the group as a whole – in raising its average quality – rather than to the individual. Only insofar as information in addition to race is used is there any incentive for training.

An additional worry is that the Office of Economic Opportunity is going to use cost-benefit analysis to evaluate its programs. For many benefits may be external. The benefit from training minority groups may arise as much from raising the average quality of the group as from raising the quality of the individual trainee; and, likewise, the returns may be distributed over the whole group rather than to the individual.

C. The costs of dishonesty

The Lemons model can be used to make some comments on the costs of dishonesty. Consider a market in which goods are sold honestly or dishonestly; quality may be represented, or it may be misrepresented. The purchaser's problem, of course, is to identify quality. The presence of people in the market who are willing to offer inferior goods tends to drive the market out of existence – as in the case of our automobile "lemons." It is this possibility that represents the major costs of dishonesty – for dishonest dealings tend to drive honest dealings out of the market. There may be potential buyers of good quality products and there may be potential sellers of such products in the appropriate price range; however, the presence of people who wish to pawn bad wares off as good wares tends to drive out the legitimate

7 G. J. Stigler, "Information and the Labor Market," *Journal of Political Economy*, Vol. 70 (Oct. 1962), Supplement, p. 104.

business. The cost of dishonesty, therefore, lies not only in the amount by which the purchaser is cheated; the cost also must include the loss incurred from driving legitimate business out of existence.

Dishonesty in business is a serious problem in underdeveloped countries. Our model gives a possible structure to this statement and delineates the nature of the "external" economies involved. In particular, in the model economy described, dishonesty, or the misrepresentation of the quality of automobiles, costs ½ unit of utility per automobile; furthermore, it reduces the size of the used car market from N to 0. We can, consequently, directly evaluate the costs of dishonesty – at least in theory.

There is considerable evidence that quality variation is greater in underdeveloped than in developed areas. For instance, the need for quality control of exports and State Trading Corporations can be taken as one indicator. In India, for example, under the Export Quality Control and Inspection Act of 1963, "about 85 per cent of Indian exports are covered under one or the other type of quality control."[8] Indian housewives must carefully glean the rice of the local bazaar to sort out stones of the same color and shape which have been intentionally added to the rice. Any comparison of the heterogeneity of quality in the street market and the canned qualities of the American supermarket suggests that quality variation is a greater problem in the East than in the West.

In one traditional pattern of development the merchants of the pre-industrial generation turn into the first entrepreneurs of the next. The best-documented case is Japan,[9] but this also may have been the pattern for Britain and America.[10] In *our* picture the important skill of the merchant is identifying the quality of merchandise; those who can identify used cars in our example and can guarantee the quality may profit by as much as the difference between type two traders' buying price and type one traders' selling price. These people are the merchants. In production these skills are equally necessary – both to be able to identify the quality of inputs and to certify the quality of

8 *The Times of India,* Nov. 10, 1967, p. 1.

9 See M. J. Levy, Jr., "Contrasting Factors in the Modernization of China and Japan," in *Economic Growth: Brazil, India, Japan,* ed. S. Kuznets *et al.* (Durham, N.C.: Duke University Press, 1955).

10 C. P. Kindleberger, *Economic Development* (New York: McGraw-Hill, 1958), p. 86.

outputs. And this is one (added) reason why the merchants may logically become the first entrepreneurs.

The problem, of course, is that entrepreneurship may be a scarce resource; no development text leaves entrepreneurship unemphasized. Some treat it as central.[11] Given, then, that entrepreneurship is scarce, there are two ways in which product variations impede development. First, the pay-off to trade is great for would-be entrepreneurs, and hence they are diverted from production; second, the amount of entrepreneurial time per unit output is greater, the greater are the quality variations.

D. Credit markets in underdeveloped countries

(1) Credit markets in underdeveloped countries often strongly reflect the operation of the Lemons Principle. In India a major fraction of industrial enterprise is controlled by managing agencies (according to a recent survey, these "managing agencies" controlled 65.7 per cent of the net worth of public limited companies and 66 per cent of total assets).[12] Here is a historian's account of the function and genesis of the "managing agency system":

> The management of the South Asian commercial scene remained the function of merchant houses, and a type of organization peculiar to South Asia known as the Managing Agency. When a new venture was promoted (such as a manufacturing plant, a plantation, or a trading venture), the promoters would approach an established managing agency. The promoters might be Indian or British, and they might have technical or financial resources or merely a concession. In any case they would turn to the agency because of its reputation, which would encourage confidence in the venture and stimulate investment.[13]

In turn, a second major feature of the Indian industrial scene has been the dominance of these managing agencies by caste (or, more accurately, communal) groups. Thus firms can usually be classified

11 For example, see W. Arthur Lewis, *The Theory of Economic Growth* (Homewood, Ill.: Irwin, 1955), p. 196.
12 *Report of the Committee on the Distribution of Income and Levels of Living,* Part I, Government of India, Planning Commission, Feb. 1964, p. 44.
13 H. Tinker, *South Asia: A Short History* (New York: Praeger, 1966), p. 134.

according to communal origin.[14] In this environment, in which outside investors are likely to be bilked of their holdings, either (1) firms
establish a reputation for "honest" dealing, which confers upon them
a monopoly rent insofar as their services are limited in supply, or (2)
the sources of finance are limited to local communal groups which
can use communal – and possibly familial – ties to encourage honest
dealing *within* the community. It is, in Indian economic history,
extraordinarily difficult to discern whether the savings of rich land-
lords failed to be invested in the industrial sector (1) because of a fear
to invest in ventures controlled by other communities, (2) because of
inflated propensities to consume, or (3) because of low rates of
return.[15] At the very least, however, it is clear that the British-owned
managing agencies tended to have an equity holding whose commu-

14 The existence of the following table (and also the small per cent of firms under
   mixed control) indicates the communalization of the control of firms. *Source:*
   M. M. Mehta, *Structure of Indian Industries* (Bombay: Popular Book Depot,
   1955), p. 314.

Distribution of industrial control by community Number of firms			
	1911	1931	1951
British	281	416	382
Parsis	15	25	19
Gujratis	3	11	17
Jews	5	9	3
Muslims	—	10	3
Bengalis	8	5	20
Marwaris	—	6	96
Mixed control	28	28	79
Total	340	510	619

Also, for the cotton industry see H. Fukuzawa, "Cotton
Mill Industry," in V. B. Singh, editor, *Economic History of India, 1857–1956* (Bombay: Allied Publishers,
1965).

15 For the mixed record of industrial profits, see D. H. Buchanan, *The Development of Capitalist Enterprise in India* (New York: Kelley, 1966, reprinted).

nal origin was more heterogeneous than the Indian-controlled agency houses, and would usually include both Indian and British investors.

(2) A second example of the workings of the Lemons Principle concerns the extortionate rates which the local moneylender charges his clients. In India these high rates of interest have been the leading factor in landlessness; the so-called "Cooperative Movement" was meant to counteract this growing landlessness by setting up banks to compete with the local moneylenders.[16] While the large banks in the central cities have prime interest rates of 6, 8, and 10 per cent, the

16 The leading authority on this is Sir Malcolm Darling. See his *Punjabi Peasant in Prosperity and Debt*. The following table may also prove instructive:

	Commonest rates for		
	Secured loans (per cent)	Unsecured loans (per cent)	Grain loans (per cent)
Punjab	6 to 12	12 to 24 (18¾ commonest)	25
United Provinces	9 to 12	24 to 37½	25 (50 in Oudh)
Bihar		18¾	50
Orissa	12 to 18¾	25	25
Bengal	8 to 12	9 to 18 for "respectable clients"	—
		18¾ to 37½ (the latter common to agriculturalists)	—
Central Provinces	6 to 12	15 for proprietors	25
		24 for occupancy tenants	—
		37½ for ryots with no right of transfer	—
Bombay	9 to 12	12 to 25 (18 commonest)	—
Sind		36	—
Madras	12	15 to 18 (in insecure tracts 24 not uncommon)	20 to 50

Source: Punjabi Peasant in Prosperity and Debt, 3rd ed. (Oxford University Press, 1932), p. 190.

local moneylender charges 15, 25, and even 50 per cent. The answer to this seeming paradox is that credit is granted only where the granter has (1) easy means of enforcing his contract or (2) personal knowledge of the character of the borrower. The middleman who tries to arbitrage between the rates of the moneylender and the central bank is apt to attract all the "lemons" and thereby make a loss.

This interpretation can be seen in Sir Malcolm Darling's interpretation of the village moneylender's power:

> It is only fair to remember that in the Indian village the moneylender is often the one thrifty person amongst a generally thriftless people; and that his methods of business, though demoralizing under modern conditions, suit the happy-go-lucky ways of the peasant. He is always accessible, even at night; dispenses with troublesome formalities, asks no inconvenient questions, advances promptly, and if interest is paid, does not press for repayment of principal. He keeps in close personal touch with his clients, and in many villages shares their occasions of weal or woe. *With his intimate knowledge of those around him he is able, without serious risk, to finance those who would otherwise get no loan at all.* [Italics added.][17]

Or look at Barbara Ward's account:

> A small shopkeeper in a Hong Kong fishing village told me: "I give credit to anyone who anchors regularly in our bay; but if it is someone I don't know well, then I think twice about it unless I can find out all about him."[18]

Or, a profitable sideline of cotton ginning in Iran is the loaning of money for the next season, since the ginning companies often have a line of credit from Teheran banks at the market rate of interest. But

17 M. Darling, *Punjabi Peasant*, p. 204.
18 B. Ward, "Cash or Credit Crops," *Economic Development and Cultural Change*, Vol. 8 (Jan. 1960), reprinted in *Peasant Society: A Reader*, ed. G. Foster *et al.* (Boston: Little, Brown and Company, 1967), quote on p. 142. In the same volume, see also G. W. Skinner, "Marketing and Social Structure in Rural China," and S. W. Mintz, "Pratik: Haitian Personal Economic Relations."

in the first years of operation large losses are expected from unpaid debts – due to poor knowledge of the local scene.[19]

IV. Counteracting institutions

Numerous institutions arise to counteract the effects of quality uncertainty. One obvious institution is guarantees. Most consumer durables carry guarantees to ensure the buyer of some normal expected quality. One natural result of our model is that the risk is borne by the seller rather than by the buyer.

A second example of an institution which counteracts the effects of quality uncertainty is the brand-name good. Brand names not only indicate quality but also give the consumer a means of retaliation if the quality does not meet expectations. For the consumer will then curtail future purchases. Often too, new products are associated with old brand names. This ensures the prospective consumer of the quality of the product.

Chains – such as hotel chains or restaurant chains – are similar to brand names. One observation consistent with our approach is the chain restaurant. These restaurants, at least in the United States, most often appear on interurban highways. The customers are seldom local. The reason is that these well-known chains offer a better hamburger than the *average* local restaurant; at the same time, the local customer, who knows his area, can usually choose a place he prefers.

Licensing practices also reduce quality uncertainty. For instance, there is the licensing of doctors, lawyers, and barbers. Most skilled labor carries some certification indicating the attainment of certain levels of proficiency. The high school diploma, the baccalaureate degree, the Ph.D., even the Nobel Prize, to some degree, serve this function of certification. And education and labor markets themselves have their own "brand names."

V. Conclusion

We have been discussing economic models in which "trust" is important. Informal unwritten guarantees are preconditions for trade and

19 Personal conversation with mill manager, April 1968.

production. Where these guarantees are indefinite, business will suffer – as indicated by our generalized Gresham's law. This aspect of uncertainty has been explored by game theorists, as in the Prisoner's Dilemma, but usually it has not been incorporated in the more traditional Arrow-Debreu approach to uncertainty.[20] But the difficulty of distinguishing good quality from bad is inherent in the business world; this may indeed explain many economic institutions and may in fact be one of the more important aspects of uncertainty.

University of California, Berkeley
Indian Statistical Institute – Planning Unit, New Delhi

20 R. Radner, "Équilibre de Marchés à Terme et au Comptant en Cas d'Incertitude," in *Cahiers d'Econometrie,* Vol. 12 (Nov. 1967), Centre National de la Recherche Scientifique, Paris.

3

The economics of caste and of the rat race and other woeful tales

I. Introduction

There is a standard model of economic behavior, the Arrow-Debreu general equilibrium model of perfect competition. While this model may not be entirely adequate as a description of economic reality, it is most useful as a standard of comparison. For in equilibrium in this model, subject to the careful qualifications of Pareto optimality, peoples' lives are as pleasurable as they possibly can be, given their tastes and productive capabilities. Consequently, to understand why peoples' lives are not as pleasurable as they might be (in the Pareto sense), it is necessary only to know why the real world fails to correspond to the Arrow-Debreu utopia.

In the real world, contrary to the assumptions of Arrow and Debreu, information is neither complete nor costless.[1] On the contrary, given the cost of information and the need for it, people typically make predictions about the behavior of the economy and the

The original version of this paper was written in the summer of 1971 and presented in seminars at Nuffield College, Oxford and Essex Universities. Sections I, II, III, and IV are taken from that original paper. Since that time some of this work has been duplicated. See Michael Spence, "Job Market Signaling," *Quarterly Journal of Economics,* LXXXVII (Aug. 1973), 355–79. Section V, on the theory of caste and its applications, was written in the summer of 1975. The author would like to thank Marcelle Arak and Daniel McFadden for valuable help and the National Science Foundation for financial support. He would also especially like to thank Michael Rothschild, the Guest Editor of this Symposium [The Economics of Information], for his many invaluable editorial comments.

1 Other approaches to the difficulties encountered by the A-D model in explaining labor markets are given by the "new" labor economics. See, for example, Doeringer, P. B. and Piore, M., *Internal Labor Markets and Manpower Analysis* (Lexington, Mass.: Heath, 1971); G. Becker, *Human Capital* (New York: Columbia University Press, 1964); and E. S. Phelps *et al., The Macroeconomic Foundations of Employment and Inflation Theory* (New York: W. W. Norton, 1970).

behavior of individuals based upon a limited number of easily observable characteristics. We say that such a prediction is based upon an *indicator;* an econometrician would call it a prediction using the method of instrumental variables. This paper shows the distortions caused to examples of the A-D (Arrow-Debreu) model by the introduction of *indicators*.

There are two types of examples of the use of *indicators* in the models that follow. One sort of *indicator* owes its existence to the potentially useful economic information provided. In the example of *sharecropping* the output produced is used as *indicator;* it serves the useful function of differentiating between farmers who have expended different levels of effort in tilling the crop. In the example of *work conditions* the speed of the assembly line predicts the ability of workers on that assembly line, and therefore differentiates workers of different ability. In contrast, in the following two examples the *indicators* owe their existence purely to social convention. In the example of *statistical discrimination,* under conditions described, all persons of the same race are predicted to have equal ability. In the example of caste the behavior of one member of society toward another is predicted by their respective caste statuses.

In this second type of example, introduction of *indicators* into the A-D model brings with it a second previously missing aspect of reality, the panoply of cultural characteristics used by anthropologists and sociologists to describe a society. For, by definition, culture consists of "regularities in the behavior, internal and external, of the members of a society, excluding those regularities which are purely hereditary."[2] Since culture concerns regularities in behavior and since subcultural membership is easy to observe, members of society, as well as visiting anthropologists and sociologists, can predict individual behavior from subcultural membership. By definition, such predictions are based on *indicators,* typical examples being predictions of behavior or ability of an individual based on his caste, class, race, sex, organizational membership, religion, friends, possessions, personal appearance, or job.

The examples are presented in detail below; each one shows the possibility, given the values of the members of the society, of an equi-

2 Quoted by Arnold Toynbee, *A Study of History, A New Edition, Revised and Abridged* (London: Oxford University Press, 1972), p. 43; from P. Bagby, *Culture and History* (London: Longmans), pp. 84 and 95.

librium that is not Pareto optimal. But before this presentation, we should also mention, at least parenthetically, another role of *indicators* in shaping society. The *indicators* by which men judge each other may warp their values and distort their goals. The anthropologists give accounts such as those of the Kwakiutl Indians, among whom the chief who burned the greatest number of blankets at feast-time, as the mark of the most conspicuous consumption, received the greatest honor.[3] The economists Galbraith and Veblen see similarity in our own consumption rites.[4]

II. Sharecropping

The first example of *indicators* deals with the simplest phenomenon. Several economists have asked why sharecropping is a common form of land system.[5] After all, since the sharecropper is much poorer than the landlord and much less liquid as well (not owning land that can be mortgaged), it would be more natural for the landlord rather than the tenant to bear the risk of crop failure. This would be accomplished if the landlord paid the tenant a wage and sold the crop (perhaps even selling some of it back to the tenant).

There is also evidence that fixed wage payments are more "natural" than sharecropping. A recent study of sharecropping in the United States South concludes that immediately following the Civil War "the wage payment system was, from all indications universally attempted."[6] Travelers' accounts seem to show that at the end of the Civil War sharecropping was viewed as an "experiment."[7]

There is, however, a very simple reason for a preference for sharecropping over a wage-payment system. There are two components to the sharecropper's input: the time he puts in and the effort expended.

3 Benedict, R., *Patterns of Culture* (Boston: Houghton Mifflin Co., 1944).

4 Veblen, T., *The Theory of the Leisure Class* (New York: Modern Library, 1934); and J. K. Galbraith, *The Affluent Society* (Boston: Houghton Mifflin Co., 1958).

5 Cheung, S. N. S., "Private Property Rights and Sharecropping," *Journal of Political Economy*, LXXVI (Nov./Dec. 1968), 1107–22. For an approach similar to that taken here, see J. E. Stiglitz, "Incentives and Risk in Sharecropping," *Review of Economic Studies*, XLI (April 1974), 219–58.

6 Ransom, R. and Sutch, R., *What Was Freedom's Price?* (New York: Cambridge University Press, forthcoming), Ch. 4.

7 *Ibid.*, Ch. 5.

While the first is easy to observe, and can be paid a fixed wage, the second cannot be observed without careful supervision of the labor.

Suppose that the input of the sharecropper depends upon his time at work and his effort; suppose further that his effort can be measured and called e. With a wage system the sharecropper should receive an income w dependent on e and t:

$$w = w(e, t).$$

Without supervision the landlord cannot determine the effort put in; and the wage paid to the individual worker will depend on the average effort of the average worker, $\bar{e}$: thus

$$w = w(\bar{e}, t).$$

This leaves no incentive to the worker for any effort beyond the minimum necessary to be paid for his time. If he dislikes effort, he will minimize it.

In contrast, in sharecropping, the farmer is paid for the effort that he puts in as well as for his time; but this effort and time are estimated imperfectly from another characteristic – the output produced. The equilibrium is distorted by this procedure, since the risk-averse farmer remains unprotected from the natural randomness inherent in agriculture.

The basic stylized facts of this model conform with the conditions of sharecropping. In traditional agriculture the hard-working farmer usually receives yields that are considerably greater than the yields of the average farmer. A Punjabi peasant, who prided himself on yields greater than those of his neighbors, once listed for me "the seven things which a good farmer does, which a poor farmer does not do." It is significant that many of these seven things involve arduous work and much patience; many are also difficult to observe.[8] A sim-

---

8 The list included the following:

1   Planting on time.
2   Using the proper inputs – seeds, fertilizers.
3   Smoothing the ground carefully before sowing, both to preserve moisture and to make irrigation easier; this involved going over the fields as many as five times with a bullock and plowboard.

ilar story has been told by John Mellor in his study of farms in a village of Uttar Pradesh.[9] Hard work generated significantly higher yields even with the use of only traditional farming methods.

The division of crops between those grown on a wage-payment system and those grown on shares is also consistent with our explanation. Where supervision is needed for reasons other than determination of effort, the model predicts that wages rather than shares will be paid. In India, for example, as an excellent rule of thumb, capital-intensive plantation crops are grown on a wage-payment system.[10] And these crops need supervision to insure cultivation.

III. Work conditions: the rat race

The second example of the use of *indicators* concerns the choice of occupation and work conditions for the selection of workers. Workers who are willing to work at a fast speed (or, equivalently for the model, under difficult work conditions) are judged to have superior abilities. The model is a complicated analog of the rat race. In the rat race the chances of getting the cheese increase with the speed of the rat, although no additional cheese is produced. In our model, unlike the rat race, workers produce more output at faster speeds; but, like the rat race, the private return for additional speed exceeds the additional output produced (faster speed results in a higher wage to the individual, not only from the return from his added production, but also because of the greater estimate of his individual ability). Furthermore, as in the rat race, the individual worker is goaded on by the knowledge that at slower speeds he must share his output with workers of lesser ability (being judged the same); similarly, he is

4 Drilling the seed to the right depth and planting in straight lines with rows of proper width. This also involved hard work with a wooden plow and considerable manual dexterity.
5 Irrigation and proper use of water.
6 Weeding often.
7 Harvesting quickly.

9 Mellor, J., *The Economics of Agricultural Development* (Ithaca, N.Y.: Cornell University Press,), Ch. 8.
10 Buchanan, D. H., *The Development of Capitalist Enterprise in India* (New York: Macmillan, 1934).

spurred on by the knowledge that at faster speeds he will share the output of workers of greater ability.

"Speed" in our model stands for "work conditions" and educational attainment.[11] In real life, wage differentials do induce persons to work under harder working conditions, and also to increase their levels of education. Likewise, it is also plausible that workers' willingness to work under harsh conditions or to obtain education is correlated positively with their productivity. (In some professions this could be reversed; good workers may demand good work conditions so that they can perform their task more satisfactorily. Perhaps chess is an example.)

A model is made to illustrate these points in the following way: good workers have a greater tolerance for poor working conditions than poor workers. Surrealistically, we picture all workers at work on some assembly line; the assembly lines, however, can work at different speeds – with three consequences: (1) the faster assembly lines require harder work and are therefore distasteful; (2) faster assembly lines produce more output; and (3) workers are faceless and nameless (in our surrealistic picture). The organization that runs the assembly line cannot tell the difference between good and bad workers, but it can perceive the average difference in quality of workers who adhere to assembly lines working at different speeds. Note that the assumption is quite realistic if unions or feelings of fairness severely restrict firms' ability to treat workers on an assembly line according to their real merit.

In our model there are N different classes of workers, numbered from 1 to N. All classes have equal population. The utility of workers of class n depends upon the goods they consume G, and the speed at which they work S. This is given by the function

$$U_n = G - S - \tfrac{3}{8}(S - n)^2, n = 1, \ldots, N.$$

Utility depends positively on the goods consumed and negatively on the speed of the assembly line. Higher grade workers are more willing to trade output for speed. The reason for the seemingly arbitrary fraction "⅜" in the utility function results from a desire to have an

11 The role of education in screening is mentioned by T. W. Schultz, *The Economic Value of Education* (New York: Columbia University Press, 1964).

equilibrium with all workers of the same class working at the same speed.

Output per worker on an assembly line depends upon its average grade of worker and also the speed at which it operates. The simplest such production function can be written

$$Q = \bar{\alpha} + S,$$

where Q is output per worker, $\bar{\alpha}$ is the average grade of worker on the assembly line, and S is the speed of the assembly line.

Capital is no constraint; and assembly lines can work at speeds S corresponding to any integer. The wage paid to each worker in equilibrium is equal to the output per worker on that assembly line.

To summarize, this is the complete specification of the economy. There are N classes of workers; there are assembly lines potentially operating at any integral speed. The solution to the economy consists of matching workers with assembly lines operating at different speeds. In equilibrium no worker will wish to move from the assembly line where he is working to an assembly line operating at a different speed.

Equilibrium. This model has the following equilibrium: Workers of type n, $n = 2, \ldots, N$, will be working at speed $n + 1$; workers of type 1 will be working at speed 1. No worker will wish to move to an assembly line working at any other speed.

Proof. The proof is given in three parts. Part I shows that a worker of index n, $n \geq 3$ has no incentive to move from an assembly line of speed $n + 1$. Part II shows that a worker of index $n = 1$ has no incentive to move from an assembly line of speed 1. Part III shows that a worker of index $n = 2$ has no incentive to move from an assembly line of speed 3.

Part I. A worker of index n, $3 \leq n \leq N - 1$ has no incentive to move. The northwest quadrant of Table I shows the utility of a type-n worker at equilibrium speed and if he moves to assembly lines one unit faster than the equilibrium $(n + 2)$, and to speeds one unit slower than equilibrium (n). Speeds more than one unit faster or slower than equilibrium can easily be shown to be outside the range

Table 1. *Utility of worker by type of worker on assembly lines at equilibrium and one unit faster and one unit slower than equilibrium*

Type of worker	Speed	Average quality	Utility	Type of worker	Speed	Average quality	Utility
$3 \leq n \leq$	n	$n - 1$	$n - 1$		N	$N - 1$	$N - 1$
$N - 1$	$n + 1$	n	$n - \frac{3}{8}$	N	$N + 1$	$N + 1$	$N - \frac{3}{8}$
	$n + 2$	$n + 1$	$n - \frac{1}{2}$		$N + 2$	N	$N - \frac{3}{4}$
	0	1	$\frac{5}{8}$		2	$1\frac{1}{8}$	$1\frac{1}{8}$
1	1	1	1	2	3	2	$1\frac{3}{8}$
	2	1	$\frac{5}{8}$		4	3	$1\frac{5}{8}$

of consideration. The northwest quadrant of Table 1 shows that a worker of type n has highest utility at speed $n + 1$. Table 1 is derived by applying the formula

$$U_n = G - S - \tfrac{3}{8}(S - n)^2 = \bar{\alpha} - \tfrac{3}{8}(S - n)^2.$$

The northeast quadrant of Table I is analogous for workers of class N. Labor of index N receives maximum utility working at speed $N + 1$.

Part II. A worker of type 1 has no incentive to move from assembly lines of speed 1. The southwest quadrant of Table I shows the utility of type 1 if he moves to speeds 0 or 2 and if he remains at speed 1. Maximum utility is obtained at $S = 1$.

Part III. A worker of type 2 has no incentive to move. If he moves to speed 2, workers of type 1 will move onto these assembly lines until the utility of type 1 workers is the same on assembly lines of speeds 1 and 2. This will occur if the average quality on assembly lines of speed 2 is $1\frac{1}{8}$. Thus, the southeast quadrant of Table I gives the utility that a worker of type 2 will enjoy at equilibrium speed $S = 3$, and at speeds one unit faster and slower. His utility is maximized at speed $S = 3$.

Comment on equilibrium. It is clear that in this solution everyone except type-1 workers is working at speeds faster than the optimum. In the absence of workers of other grades, each type of worker n would work at speed n, receiving utility in amount n. The solution is nonoptimal because each grade of worker (except for the lowest) works at a faster speed than in the absence of other workers – since each grade of worker wishes to avoid sharing its output with workers of lower grade. Workers increase their speed so as to winnow out poorer grades.

If the government places a tax on assembly lines of one unit per worker per unit speed, all workers will work at speed n. (This is easy to see by reconstruction of Table I with workers of type n working at speed n and a tax on work at speed n equal to n. For $n \leqq N - 1$, workers of type n receive 0 utility at speed n. If they move to assembly lines one unit faster or one unit slower, they receive utility $-$ ⅜.) Since any redistribution of the taxes collected will leave the social rate of transformation of goods for speed equal to the marginal rate of substitution of goods for speed for each worker, such redistributions are Pareto optimal.

IV. Statistical discrimination

In the first two examples the *indicators* chosen have arisen for reasons of technology and production. They are used for natural economic reasons, given the utility functions, the production functions, and the technology of obtaining information. In the next two examples the *indicators* chosen are based instead on social groupings whose existence is totally independent of utility functions, production functions, or information technology. The first two examples showed how *indicators* of natural origin caused distortions to marginal principles. The next two examples show how *indicators* of social origin may lead the economy into a low-level equilibrium trap.

We begin with Arrow's model[12] of *statistical discrimination* (perhaps already familiar to the reader). In this example, under some

---

12 Arrow, K. J., "Models of Job Discrimination," and "Some Mathematical Models of Race in the Labor Market," Chs. 2 and 6, in A. H. Pascal, ed., *Racial Discrimination in Economic Life* (Lexington: Heath, 1972). The model here is different in important detail from the original by Arrow, who does not consider the two equivalent. I am sure that he would agree that, however the mathematics differ, the economic spirit of the two models is the same.

circumstances, employers use the average quality of a given race to predict the quality of individuals of that race. It is easy to see that if such an *indicator* is used, it will destroy all incentive for self-improvement for that race, since all individuals of the race are judged the same and therefore paid the same wage irrespective of individual merit. In this way prejudice may produce a lower level equilibrium trap: if a race is deemed by prejudice to be unqualified, no incentive is given to become qualified, and the prophecy is self-fulfilling.

The model

In this model there are just two types of jobs, one requiring qualified labor and the other requiring either qualified or unqualified labor. It is costly to test workers individually to see whether or not they are qualified. The change in proportion of qualified workers depends upon the incentives for self-improvement, which are differences in wages for qualified and unqualified workers of that race.

With slight modification of Arrow's notation and also of his equations, these assumptions lead to the following model. Let f_u be the marginal product of unqualified labor; f_q be the marginal product of qualified labor; let P_R be the proportion of race R predicted to be qualified. Let r be the cost spent per period to determine whether an individual worker is qualified. Let $\dot{P}_R$ be the change in the proportion of qualified workers of race R. The newly qualified of race R depends upon the differential in wages paid to qualified and unqualified workers of that race. The rate of retirement of that race is λ, so we can write $\dot{P}_R$ as

$$\dot{P}_R = \phi(w_{qR} - w_{uR}) - \lambda P_R,$$

where w_{qR} is the wage paid to qualified members of race R, and w_{uR} is the wage paid to unqualified members of race R.

If the expected costs of testing a worker of a given race exceed the difference in marginal products of qualified and unqualified workers, no worker will be tested, and all workers of that race will be used in unqualified jobs. Thus, competitive firms, earning zero profits, will pay wages

$$w_{qR} = \max\left(f_q - r/P_R, f_u\right)$$
$$w_{uR} = f_u,$$

and $\dot{P}_R$ becomes

$$\dot{P}_R = \phi \, (\max \, (f_q - r/P_R - f_u, \, 0)) - \lambda P_R.$$

If $\phi(0)$ is small (i.e., less than $\lambda r/(f_q - f_u)$), P_R has a locally stable low-level equilibrium equal to $\phi(0)/\lambda$.

There are, however, some difficulties in applying this model to real-world racial discrimination. The costliness of testing workers' qualifications suggests that the traits necessary for qualification must also be difficult to observe.[13] Arrow is specific in this regard: "I am thinking here not of the conventional type of education or experience, which is easily observable, but more subtle types the employer cannot observe directly: the habits of action and thought that favor good performance in skilled jobs–steadiness, punctuality, responsiveness, and initiative."[14] Indeed, there is considerable evidence of the importance of these four qualities for job success.[15] But is it also true, as implied by the equation for $\dot{P}_R$, that these "habits of thought and action" are acquired in response to wage differentials? Psychologists seem to believe that most fundamental personality traits are learned at an early age.[16] If they are correct, the low-level trap will occur only if schooling and child-rearing techniques are responsive to wage incentives.

13 There is also the possibility that tests that are available for whites are not available for blacks. A recent Berkeley Ph.D. thesis reports that, although a group of blacks were more consistent in their answers to a long questionnaire than a group of whites, nevertheless, their IQ scores were significantly lower. See L. Dunn, "Labor Supply for Southern Industrialization," Ph.D. thesis, University of California, Berkeley, 1974, pp. 298 and 301.

14 Arrow, "Models of Job Discrimination," p. 97.

15 The essays in the book edited by Peter Doeringer, *Programs to Aid the Disadvantaged* (Englewood Cliffs, N.J.: Prentice-Hall, 1969), repeatedly and emphatically mention the importance of punctual and steady job attendance. E. Banfield in *The Unheavenly City* (Boston: Little, Brown and Company, p. 143) cites the findings of the Coleman Report that for blacks, *attitude* was the most important determinant for school success.

16 See Erik Erikson, *Childhood and Society* (New York: W. W. Norton, 1956, 1963).

V. Caste and group organizations

Whether or not statistical discrimination in the fashion of Arrow is directly applicable to racial discrimination, his model is appealing in at least one respect. It differs fundamentally from the previous models of Becker[17] and Welch,[18] in which discrimination is explained by tastes. In these models any individual with positive taste for discrimination will receive positive economic rewards for reducing this taste. Thus in the Becker-Welch models discrimination persists *despite* economic incentives. In contrast, in Arrow's example discrimination exists at least partially because of economic incentives.

It may appear that the tastes of persons in discriminating societies are so overwhelmingly biased in favor of discrimination that, relatively, the positive or negative effects of economic incentive are of only minor moment. But this ignores the broad historical perspective, which attempts to explain the stability (or disappearance) of institutions over a long period of time. For there are a fair number of cases where opportunities have arisen for deviants to break the caste code and make economic profits, with consequent rise in their social position and erosion of the caste taboos. Consider three diverse examples of this phenomenon. In Japan as merchants have become more economically successful, so too have the taboos against trade and manufacture been reduced.[19] Even in caste-bound India caste status rises with the economic success of the caste, although, typically, newly successful castes also adjust their social customs, at least partially, to reflect their higher status.[20] The best example of economic

17 Becker, G., *The Economics of Discrimination* (Chicago: University of Chicago Press, 1969).

18 Welch, F., "Labor-Market Discrimination: Extrapolation of Income Differences in the Rural South," *Journal of Political Economy*, LXXV (Aug. 1967), 584–96.

19 See, for example, Marion Levy, "Contrasting Factors in the Modernization of China and Japan," in S. Kuznets *et al.*, eds., *Economic Growth: Brazil, India, Japan* (Durham, N.C.: Duke University Press, 1955).

20 See M. N. Srinivas, *Social Change in Modern India* (Berkeley: University of California Press, 1967), pp. 7–8. For a detailed description of the upgrading of one caste and its links with economic opportunity, see Oscar Lewis, *Village Life in India* (New York: Vintage Books, 1965), pp. 70–77. It is clear that this caste would have found it much more difficult to upgrade its caste status in the absence of economic opportunities outside its village.

success reducing taboos is, most probably, the elimination of the sanctions against collection of interest. The usurer of the Middle Ages
has turned into the banker of today.

This section introduces a new class of models in which, as in
Arrow's statistical-discrimination equilibrium trap, those who break
caste customs suffer economically. This class of models depends upon
an important facet of caste societies missing in previous models of
discrimination. In previous models current transactions (so long as
they are legal) do not result in changed relations with uninvolved
parties in subsequent transactions.[21] For example, if farmer X makes
a contract for sale of wheat to speculator Y, his subsequent dealings
with speculator Z will be unaffected. On the contrary, in a caste society any transaction that breaks the caste taboos changes the subsequent behavior of uninvolved parties toward the caste-breakers. To
take an extreme example, consider what would happen if a Brahman
should knowingly hire an outcaste cook: the Brahman would be outcasted, and the cook would find subsequent employment almost
impossible to obtain.

The possible intervention of third parties in a transaction allows
for a richer class of *indicators* than that given by Arrow's statistical
discrimination – typically, the use of *indicators* in caste societies being
less narrowly technological. Generally, in a caste society if a member
of caste A relates to a member of caste B in a given way, he can
predict from knowledge of the relations between caste A and caste B
how members of all castes will relate to him in future transactions.
Such predictions can lead to an equilibrium in which all expectations
are met and economic incentives favor obedience to the caste code –
even in the extreme case where tastes are totally neutral regarding
the observance of caste customs.

The following three conditions describe marriage customs in
India.[22]

1. Society is divided into mutually exclusive groups (called castes).

2. A code of behavior dictates how members of these castes should
behave. Regarding marriage there are complicated rules as to who

---

21 Note that one aspect of magic and taboo is that persons or events uninvolved in
the Western sense, may be involved by *contagious or homeopathic magic*. See
Sir James G. Frazer, *The Golden Bough* (New York: St. Martins, 1936).

22 A good account of caste marriage customs is given in J. H. Hutton, *Caste in
India* (Oxford University Press, Fourth Edition, 1961).

may marry whom, payment of the dowry, the timing and performance of the marriage rites, etc. The caste rules dictate not only the
code of behavior, but also the punishment for infractions: violators
will be outcasted; furthermore, those who fail to treat outcastes as
dictated by caste code will themselves be outcasted.

3. Caste members predict that those who do not follow the caste
code will be made outcastes and will receive the treatment of the average outcaste. An outcaste in India is permitted to hold only scavenging (or other polluting) jobs. He is not allowed to eat with caste members, to touch them, or to touch their food, which in the case of
someone outcasted includes his own parents and siblings. Of course,
his own children will be outcastes and will suffer the same
prohibitions.

Why should these three conditions describing marriage customs in
India be of interest to the economist? First, note that those who fail
to follow, or even to enforce the caste customs do not gain the profits
of the successful arbitrageur but instead suffer the stigma of the outcaste. If the punishment of becoming an outcaste is predicted to be
sufficiently severe, the system of caste is held in equilibrium irrespective of individual tastes, by economic incentives; the predictions
of the caste system become a self-fulfilling prophecy.[23]

Second, the recent extensions of the model of supply and demand
to discrimination, household organization, crime and marriage show
that the boundaries between sociology and economics are by no
means clear; if economic models can explain sociological phenomena,
so also the process can work in reverse with sociological models
describing economic phenomena. With appropriate adjustment, the
model of marriage in India explains both economies pathologically
different from the A-D utopia, and also special pathologies in economies in which perfect competition, or slight deviations therefrom,
are the norm.

Finally, the formal model of caste equilibrium works sponta-
neously without direction of any individual or organization. But in
this model it is also natural to have the exact same economic structure
with some arbiter of the caste code. Indeed the model is therefore

23 Note that this is the "terrorist" model of economic activity. One good example
is the terrorist regime of Henry V of England, described by G. Mattingly, *Cath-
erine of Aragon* (New York: Random House Paperback, 1960). Note also that
this model describes the college "honors" systems.

useful in indicating how individuals and organizations can wield great powers – quite possibly, as in some of the later examples, with considerable abuse.

Formal model of caste equilibrium

This subsection presents a formal model of caste equilibrium. Caste equilibrium is defined as a state of the economy in which caste customs are obeyed, yet no single individual, by behaving differently, can make himself better off. The first concern is, of course, to describe this equilibrium. However, since there are also coalitions of individuals who by acting together can make themselves better off than in equilibrium, it is also of interest to know the relative ease or difficulty of forming such a coalition. For this purpose we also look at the size and nature of the smallest equilibrium-breaking coalition.

Four sets of assumptions describe the economy: those describing technology, market structures, tastes, and the social system. The assumptions describing the social system are laid out in parallel with the earlier description of marriage in India. In general this model is extremely simple, subject to one complication. By its very nature the caste system involves trade and the division of labor. If outcastes could set up their own economy independent of caste members, the caste system would fall apart. Therefore, three assumptions are inserted that lead individuals to trade with one another: laborers can produce only one product; firms produce only one product; and tastes are such that persons will wish to purchase more than one good.

Technology T1. There are three types of jobs: skilled jobs, unskilled jobs, and scavenging jobs. (Subscripts sk, u, and sc refer to *sk*illed, *un*skilled and *sc*avenging, respectively.)

T2. There are n different products, labeled $i = 1, \ldots, n$.

T3. The production of each product depends upon the quantity of labor employed and the jobs performed by the labor. Let θ_{sk}, θ_u, and θ_{sc} denote the output of one unit of labor in producing any product in a skilled job, unskilled job, or scavenging job, respectively. The production function of good i is then

$$q_i = \sum_j \theta_j n_{ij},$$

where

$$j = sk, u, sc, i = 1, \ldots, n$$
q_i = output of product i, and
n_{ij} = quantity of labor employed in job type j in production of good i.

Of course,

(1) $\theta_{sc} < \theta_u < \theta_{sk}$.

T4. Because of economies due to specialization workers can work on the production of only one product.

Market structures. All firms are competitive profit maximizers. These firms can produce only one product. They hire labor and sell output on the market. A firm is willing to bid for labor the expected marginal value product of that labor.

Tastes. All persons have the same utility function U, which is independent of the caste code.

(2) $U = \sum_{i=1}^{n} \min(x_i, \alpha),$

where x_i is consumption of good i and α is a parameter of the utility function.

Social Structure S1. By birth there are just two castes divided into a dominant caste D and a nondominant caste N. Labor of both castes D and N can be outcasted. Outcastes, if any, form a third group.

S2. The caste code dictates that D labor may work in only skilled jobs; N labor may work in only unskilled jobs; and outcaste labor may only hold scavenging jobs. The caste code also says that all persons who purchase from firms not using labor according to the caste code will themselves be outcasted.

S3. Persons predict that breakers of the caste code will be outcasted and receive the wages bid for outcaste labor.

Caste equilibrium. Let the economy be described as above. Let w_k, $k = D, N$ denote the wage of caste k. Let p_i denote the price of good i produced by firms that use labor according to the caste code. Let good 1 be the numeraire good, with price equal to 1. Assume parameter values

(3) $\alpha < (\theta_u - \theta_{sc})/(1 - \theta_{sc}/\theta_{sk})$

and

(4) $n > \theta_{sk}/\alpha.$

The following describe an equilibrium with fulfilled expectations:

1. $w_D = \theta_{sk}, w_N = \theta_u.$
2. The price of all goods produced by firms using labor according to caste code is 1.
3. There are no outcastes. N labor works at unskilled jobs. D labor works at skilled jobs.
4. Utility of D labor is θ_{sk}; utility of N labor is θ_u.
5. The highest wage bid for outcaste labor is θ_{sc}.

A coalition of k^* firms, producing k^* different products and using outcaste labor in skilled jobs, can break this equilibrium if

$$k^* > (\theta_u - \theta_{sc})/\alpha(1 - \theta_{sc}/\theta_{sk}).$$

Proof. It is obvious that the described equilibrium is feasible. We need show only that no new firm can make zero or positive profits and bid a higher wage either for N labor or for outcaste labor.

N labor. Suppose that a new firm bids a higher wage for N labor than θ_u. It must use some of this labor in skilled jobs. In this case its profits per laborer will not exceed

$$p\theta_{sk} - \theta_u,$$

where p is the price received for its product. If profits are nonnegative,

$$p \geqq \theta_u/\theta_{sk}.$$

But at a price as great as θ_u/θ_{sk} this firm will have no customers. Consider a prospective customer. This customer will be outcasted because N labor is used in skilled jobs. Therefore, his expected wage is θ_{sc}. He will maximize expected utility by purchasing α units at a price p and $(\theta_{sc} - \alpha p)$ units of other goods from other firms that use labor according to the caste code.

His total utility will therefore be

(5) $\quad \theta_{sc} - \alpha p + \alpha \leqq \theta_{sc} - \alpha \theta_u/\theta_{sk} + \alpha.$

But by (1) and (3) the right-hand side of (5) is less than θ_u.

Since the customer of this firm receives utility at least as large as θ_u if he does not purchase from the caste-breaking firm, the demand for the firm's products will be zero.

Outcaste labor. No firm can bid a wage higher than θ_{sc} for outcaste labor and receive a profit if this bid is accepted. For a firm to pay a higher wage than θ_{sc}, it must employ outcaste labor in skilled or unskilled jobs. Its profits per laborer will not exceed

$p\theta_{sk} - \theta_{sc}.$

If profits are nonnegative,

$p \geqq \theta_{sc}/\theta_{sk}.$

But at a price as great as θ_{sc}/θ_{sk} the firm will have no customers: any prospective customer will be outcasted and expect to receive a wage θ_{sc}. Consider this customer. He will buy α units from this firm at a price p and will purchase $(\theta_{sc} - \alpha p)$ units of other goods from other firms. Therefore, his utility will be no greater than

(6) $\quad \theta_{sc} - \alpha \theta_{sc}/\theta_{sk} + \alpha.$

But since (6) is less than θ_u by (3), this firm will have no customers. Hence the maximum bid for outcaste labor will be θ_{sc}.

Equilibrium-breaking coalition

Finally, a coalition of k^* firms, $k^* > (\theta_u - \theta_{sc})/\alpha(1 - \theta_{sc}/\theta_{sk})$, can break the equilibrium. Such firms can offer a wage bid θ_{sc} for outcaste labor, and offer to sell their output at a price θ_{sc}/θ_{sk}. The expected utility of a person purchasing from these firms will be

$$\min\ (\theta_{sk},\ \theta_{sc} - k^*\alpha\ \theta_{sc}/\theta_{sk} + k^*\alpha),$$

which is greater than θ_u if $k^* > (\theta_u - \theta_{sc})/\alpha(1 - \theta_{sc}/\theta_{sk})$. Thus the coalition of firms will be able to attract customers; and since workers will be better off receiving θ_{sc} in wages and purchasing from firms that break the caste code, these firms will also be able to attract workers.

Comments on caste equilibrium

1. The equilibrium described has two types of distortion due to caste structure. The equilibrium is not Pareto-optimal, since in a Pareto-optimal equilibrium N workers would work in skilled jobs, for which they are fully qualified. Also, income distribution is skewed along caste lines, since in the absence of caste all workers would receive the same wage.

2. There is another equilibrium, also with fulfilled expectations, in which all workers work in skilled jobs and receive a wage θ_{sk}. The price of all goods is 1.

3. The smallest equilibrium-breaking coalition is the smallest group that can set themselves up as a separate subsector and be as well off as in equilibrium while trading with caste members on the terms of trade granted to outcastes.

In situations where this coalition must be large, where trade with the caste economy is necessary, or where the cost of forming a coalition is high, the threat to equilibrium of such a coalition is small. These principles are illustrated in the examples that follow.

Three examples of caste equilibrium

Example 1. Racial discrimination. Racial discrimination is implicit in the model, the major difference between the caste model and those of Becker, Welch, and Arrow[24] being in the assumption

---

24 Arrow, "Models of Job Discrimination" and "Some Mathematical Models"; Becker, "Economics of Discrimination"; Welch, "Labor-Market Discrimination."

that persons use race to predict how everyone else will react to hiring persons of different races in different jobs. Their predictions result in a lower level equilibrium trap in which all predictions are met.[25]

Example 2. Government-business groups. Allegedly many government-business groups, including the military-industrial state, governmental regulator-regulatee nexuses and political machines are held together by a caste-outcaste structure similar to that of our model. By nature the important operations of these groups are usually secret[26] or too technical for unambiguous assessment; but there are some recent and exceptional accounts of the detailed operation of particular political machines.[27]

The example of Robert Moses, the construction boss of New York City of long duration, illustrates especially well the applicability of the model. The story of Moses, like all such tales of powerful men, is in many ways unique – but his system of control through outcasting exactly corresponds to our model. There were a large variety of statuses in the Moses machine (from personal aide to Mayor of New York City); but it was clear to all concerned that disobedience to the boss's dictates regarding construction would lead to outcasting from the machine. For the politician, this meant loss of campaign funds and of the construction pork barrel and, consequently, the almost certain loss of his next election; for engineers it meant loss of jobs. Furthermore, it is reported, persons who failed to respect the outcaste status of those in Moses's disfavor were in turn threatened, becoming

25 Certainly our model gives a good first approximation to the apartheid system in South Africa. See A. Lewis, "South Africa: The End Is Inevitable But Not Predictable," *New York Times Magazine,* September 21, 1975.

26 A recent incident epitomizes bureaucratic attitudes toward public disclosure. Alexander Butterfield, the bureaucrat whose own disclosure toppled the Nixon administration, wrote a memorandum to Haldeman regarding A. Ernest Fitzgerald, the government cost accountant who was fired after disclosing the Lockheed C-5A cost overruns. "Let him bleed a little," wrote Butterfield. According to the *New York Times Magazine,* Butterfield felt justified because "he considered Fitzgerald disloyal for not confining his reports to Air Force channels." A. R. Smith, "The Butterfield Exchange," *New York Times Magazine,* July 20, 1975.

27 See T. Harry Williams, *Huey Long* (New York: Knopf, 1969); R. A. Caro, *The Power Broker: Robert Moses and the Fall of New York City* (New York: Knopf, 1974); and paperback, (New York: Vintage, Random House, 1974).

themselves the subjects of Moses's abuse and threats.[28] The uniqueness of Moses lay largely in his perfection of the system – mainly in his use of interlocking jobs to threaten the elected officials responsible for his reappointments and also in his use of the Triborough Bridge Authority (whose files, by a Moses-engineered legal quirk, were closed to public scrutiny) to maintain secret dossiers.

While the Moses example is extreme, it shows that in cases where public authority is delegated and cannot be easily scrutinized from outside, a caste-outcaste mechanism can arise that keeps the use of the authority secret while the resources are used for private aims. Because of the secrecy of such operations ipso facto, the importance of such misallocations for the distribution of income and of power is impossible to assess.

Example 3. Professional groups. A final example (or set of examples) of the caste-class equilibrium occurs in professional groups. The public often delegates authority to professional organizations to police their own members – the most prominent of these being bar and medical associations. In turn, the members are expected to maintain professional conduct. Since cooperation with others in the profession is a necessary part of the job, the same outcasting mechanism used by caste, races, and government-business cliques enforces a professional unanimity that gives the profession more than its fair share of economic power.

VI. Conclusions

Our four woeful tales have described the ways in which the use of *indicators* can distort equilibrium. In so doing, we have also answered two challenges to economic theory.

The standard individualistic theories of income distribution and resource allocation are notable by the absence of variables describing social structure, except insofar as these variables affect exogenously

28 See Caro's rather blunt description of Moses's style of operation: "Within a remarkably brief time after Moses entered the City Administration word spread through City Hall and the Municipal Building that any time anyone got in Moses's way Moses kicked him in the. . . . So the men who worked in the two buildings were in general exceedingly careful not to get in his way, they went to great lengths to do exactly what he wanted – when he wanted."

given tastes or the initial allocation bundles. The absence of these variables poses the first challenge: to construct an individualistic theory in which income distribution and resource allocation reflect, to some extent, the divisions of society as described by the sociologists. The most common *indicators* are based upon the standard subcultural divisions of a society. And, as a result, the use of *indicators* makes equilibrium income distribution and resource allocation dependent on these divisions; and the first challenge is answered.

The second challenge to economic theory concerns the relation between marginalism and social custom. As long as most persons have positive utility for obeying social customs, and as long as activities are pursued up to the point where marginal costs equal marginal benefits, there will be rewards for breaking social customs insofar as they fail to promote economic efficiency. While such rewards occur sometimes, and they may also be spectacular, I would tend to believe that usually the greatest returns go to those who do not break social customs. Archetypically, they join the proper fraternity, work for the proper law firm, and may even marry the boss's daughter. In a segregationist society, such persons discriminate; in a caste society they follow the caste code. While not denying the possible returns to the arbitrageur and social deviant, the models of statistical discrimination and caste explain why economic rewards may favor those who follow prevailing social custom; and in so doing, they give economic reasons why such social customs may endure.

University of California, Berkeley

4

The economics of "tagging" as applied to the optimal income tax, welfare programs, and manpower planning

The advantages of a negative income tax are easy to describe. Such a tax typically gives positive work incentives to even the poorest persons. With some forms of the negative income tax there are no incentives for families to split apart to obtain greater welfare payments. Furthermore, individuals of similar income are treated in similar fashion, and therefore it is fair and also relatively cheap and easy to administer.

In contrast to these advantages of a negative income tax, the advantages of a system of welfare made up of a patchwork of different awards to help various needy groups are less easy to describe and also less well understood. Such a system uses various characteristics, such as age, employment status, female head of household, to identify (in my terminology to "tag") groups of persons who are on the average needy. These groups are then given special treatment, or, as the economist would view it, they are given a special tax schedule different from the rest of the populace. A system of tagging permits relatively high welfare payments with relatively low marginal rates of taxation, a proposition which will be explained presently and discussed at some length.

I

It is the aim of this paper to explore the nature of the optimal negative income tax with tagging and to compare this tax with the optimal negative income tax in which all groups are treated alike. I should emphasize at the outset, however, that I do not wish to defend one type of welfare system versus another – rather, I feel that if wel-

I am indebted to George Borts and an anonymous referee for invaluable comments. I would also like to thank the National Science Foundation for research support under grant number SOC 75-23076, administered by the Institute of Business and Economic Research, University of California-Berkeley.

fare reform is to be successful, the merits of different systems must be understood, especially the merits of the system which is to be replaced. The evidence is fairly strong that the proponents of welfare reform have failed to understand (or to face) the costs involved in going from a system of welfare based on tagging (such as we now have in the United States) to one which treats all people uniformly.

The role of tagging in income redistribution can be seem most simply in a very simple formula and its modification. Consider a negative income tax of the form $T = -\alpha\overline{Y} + tY$, where α is the fraction of per capita income received by a person with zero gross income, t is the marginal rate of taxation, and $\overline{Y}$ is per capita income. Summing the left-hand side and the right-hand side of this formula over all individuals in the economy and dividing by total income yields a formula of the form:

(1) $t = \alpha + g$

where g is the ratio of net taxes collected to total income, and t and α come from the formula for the negative income tax.[1] Formula (1) indicates the fundamental tradeoff involved in income redistribution by a linear negative income tax. Higher levels of support α can be given, but only at the cost of higher marginal rates of taxation. Thus, if α is 40 percent and g is 15 percent, numbers which are not unrealistic, marginal tax rates are 55 percent.

---

1 Define g as: $\Sigma T_i/\Sigma Y_i$, where g is net tax collections relative to total income. Formula (1) can be derived as follows: $T_i = -\alpha\overline{Y} + tY_i$ is the taxes paid by individual i. Summing over all i individuals (assumed to be n in number),

(a) $\displaystyle\sum_{i=1}^{n} T_i = \sum_{i=1}^{n} -\alpha\overline{Y} + \sum_{i=1}^{n} tY_i = -\alpha n\overline{Y} + t\sum_{i=1}^{n} Y_i$

Because $\overline{Y}$ is by definition, $(\Sigma Y_i)/n$, and because g is by definition, $\sum_{i=1}^{n} T_i / \sum_{i=1}^{n} Y_i$, a division of the left-hand and the right-hand sides of (a) by ΣY_i yields:

$$\frac{\Sigma T_i}{\Sigma Y_i} = -\alpha\,\frac{n\overline{Y}}{\Sigma Y_i} + t$$

whence: $g = -\alpha + t$, and $t = \alpha + g$.

Suppose, however, that it is possible to identify (tag) a group which contains all the poor people and that this group contains only a fraction β of the total population. By giving this tagged group a minimum support, which is a fraction α of average income and a marginal tax rate t, and by giving untagged persons a zero support level and the same marginal tax rate t, similar to formula (1), we find:[2]

$$(2) \quad t = \beta\alpha + g$$

---

2 Formula (2) is derived in similar fashion to formula (1). Let n_p denote the number of poor people, with $n_p/n = \beta$. (Let poor people be numbered 1 to n_p.) Poor people pay a tax

$$T_i = (-\alpha\overline{Y} + tY_i)\, i = 1, \ldots, n_p$$

whereas other people pay a tax

$$T_i = tY_i\, i = n_p + 1, \ldots, n$$

Thus, total net revenues are:

$$\sum_{i=1}^{n} T_i = \sum_{i=1}^{n_p} (-\alpha\overline{Y} + tY_i) + \sum_{i=n_p+1}^{n} tY_i$$

and

$$\sum_{i=1}^{n} T_i = -n_p\alpha\overline{Y} + t\sum_{i=1}^{n} Y_i$$

or using the definition of β, $n_p = \beta n$

$$(b) \quad \sum_{i=1}^{n} T_i = -\beta\alpha n\overline{Y} + t\sum_{i=1}^{n} Y_i$$

Dividing the left-hand and right-hand sides of (b) by ΣY_i yields:

$$\frac{\sum_{i=1}^{n} T_i}{\sum_{i=1}^{n} Y_i} = -\beta\alpha\frac{n\overline{Y}}{\sum_{i=1}^{n} Y_i} + t$$

or $g = -\beta\alpha + t$.

Formula (2) shows that tagging makes the tradeoff between levels of support and marginal rates of taxation more favorable by eliminating the grant to taxpayers, and thus allows greater support for the poor with less distortion of the tax structure.

Table 1 is taken from the 1974 *Economic Report of the President* (p. 168). This table indicates the scope and magnitude, and also the importance, of tagging in federal redistribution programs. Such programs as aid to the aged, the blind, and the disabled, and also Medicare (including such aid administered by the Social Security system), are examples of tagging. Such programs as aid to families with dependent children are less clearcut – but it must be remembered that this program began as Aid to Dependent Children, and assistance was given to families with children without able-bodied fathers.

Female-headed households have a particularly high incidence of poverty, and this criterion (despite its perverse incentive to families to split up) was therefore one of the most efficient techniques of tagging. Other programs, such as Medicaid and housing subsidies, represent a form of tagging most common in underdeveloped and Communist countries. Since poor people spend a greater fraction of their income on some items than others, the subsidization of items of inferior but utilitarian quality constitutes one method of income "redistribution." It is also an example of tagging. In sum, Table 1 shows, to a fairly good degree of accuracy, that *U.S.* federal redistribution schemes are, with some exceptions, based on tagging.

Furthermore, the record of the debate on welfare reform reveals that the central issues involve the tradeoffs between α, t, and β reflected in formulas (1) and (2). Recall that, in August 1969, President Nixon proposed the Family Assistance Plan. By this plan a typical welfare family would receive $1,600 per year if it earned no income at all (*New York Times,* Aug. 9, 1969). There would be no decrease in benefits for the first $720 earned, but thereafter a 50¢ decline in benefits for every dollar earned up to an income of $3,920. The debate on this proposal in Congress was long and discussed many peripheral questions, but one central issue stands out. On the one side were those, with Senator Abraham Ribicoff as the leading protagonist, who considered the benefits too "meager" (Ribicoff's phrase, *New York Times,* Apr. 21, 1970); on the other side was the administration, with a succession of secretaries of Health, Education, and Welfare as leading protagonists, who viewed any increase in these benefits as too "costly" (Elliott Richardson's phrase, *New York*

Table 1. *Federal government transfer programs, fiscal year 1973*

Program	Total expenditure (millions of dollars)	Number of recipients (thousands)	Monthly benefits per recipient[a]	Percent of recipients in poverty[b]
Social Security				
Old age and survivors insurance	42,170	25,205	$139	16
Disability insurance	5,162	3,272	132	24
Public assistance				
Aid to families with dependent children	3,617	10,980	c	76
Blind	56	78	c	62
Disabled	766	1,164	c	73
Aged	1,051	1,917	c	60
Other cash programs				
Veterans' compensation and benefits	1,401	7,203	74	(4)
Unemployment insurance benefits	4,404	5,409	68	(4)
In kind				
Medicare	9,039	10,600	71	17
Medicaid	4,402	23,537	c	70
Food stamps	2,136	12,639	14	92
Public housing	1,408	3,319	c	d
Rent supplements	106	373	24	d
Homeownership assistance (section 235)	282	1,647	14	d
Rental housing assistance (section 236)	170	513	28	d

[a]The number of recipients is for individuals, not families.
[b]Poverty is defined relative to money income and the size of the recipient's family. Money income includes money transfer payments but excludes income received in kind. All percents are estimated.
[c]Programs with federal-state sharing of expenses.
[d]Not available.

Times, July 22, 1971). By this it was meant that with such an increase the marginal tax rate t would have to be too great. No compromise was reached, and in March 1972 the bill was withdrawn by the administration. In the background, of course, was the current welfare system, whose tagging programs allow a better tradeoff between α and t – even though other incentives such as incentives to work and to maintain a family may be perverse.

Thus, formula (1) and its modification with tagging are instructive and pertain to real issues. These formulas are generally useful in showing the two-way tradeoff between welfare support and marginal rates of taxation, and the three-way tradeoff between these two variables and tagging. It is fairly intuitive by consumer's surplus arguments that the cost of a tax is the "dead-weight loss" due to the gap created between private and social marginal products, which in this case is the marginal rate of taxation itself; ideally, however, the welfare cost of a tax is endogenous and should be derived from basic principles of utility maximization and general equilibrium analysis.

Ray Fair and James Mirrlees have developed the theory of the negative income tax uniformly applied. Their approach is reviewed in the next section, because, with added complication, the tradeoffs may be applied to a model of the optimal negative income tax with tagging. Section III illustrates the proposition that tagging of poor people typically results in greater support levels of the poor. Section IV gives a complicated and generalized model of optimal income redistribution with tagging, of which Section III presented a simple but illustrative example. Section V discusses the relation between tagging and the estimation of costs and benefits of manpower programs. Section VI gives conclusions.

II. A simple example and explanation of Mirrlees-Fair

Following the example of Mirrlees and Fair, there is a population with a distribution of abilities a, according to the distribution function $f(a)$. Members of this population receive income dependent on their marginal products of the form $w(a)L(a)$, where $w(a)$ is the wage of a worker of ability of index a, and $L(a)$ is the labor input of such a worker. After-tax income is $w(a)L(a) - t(w(a)L(a))$, where $t(y)$ is the tax paid on gross income y. Members of this population have utility positively dependent on after-tax income and negatively dependent on labor input. Thus, utility of a person of ability a is

(3) $\quad u(a) = u[w(a)L(a) - t(w(a)L(a)), L(a)]$

The optimal tax is defined as maximizing the expected value of the utility of the population, denoted U,

(4) $\quad U = \int u[w(a)L(a) - t(w(a)L(a)), L(a)]f(a)da$

subject to the constraint that taxes equal transfers, or,

(5) $\quad \int t(w(a)L(a))f(a)da = 0$

and also subject to the constraint that each individual chooses his labor input to maximize his utility, given the wage rate paid to persons of his ability, his utility function u, and the tax schedule $t(y)$, yielding the first-order condition:

$$\frac{\partial}{\partial L(a)} \{u[w(a)L(a) - t(w(a)L(a)), L(a)]\} = 0$$

However complicated the equations or the mathematics, the basic tradeoff made in the choice of an optimal Mirrlees-Fair style income tax can be explained as follows. As taxes are raised and incomes are redistributed, there is a gain in welfare, because income is distributed to those who have greater need of it (higher marginal utility). But this gain must be balanced against a loss: as tax rates rise in relatively productive jobs and as subsidies rise in relatively unproductive jobs, workers are less willing to take the productive (and more willing to take the unproductive) jobs. Such switching, per se, results in a loss in U because each worker is choosing the amount of work, or the kind of job, which maximizes his private utility rather than the amount of work or kind of job which maximizes social utility. In general, the redistributive gains versus the losses caused by tax/transfer-induced switching is the major tradeoff in the theory of optimal income taxes and welfare payments – both with and without tagging.

III. A simple example of optimal taxes and subsidies with tagging

Section I gave formula (2), which indicated that tagging improved the relation between the marginal tax rate and the minimum subsidy to *tagged* poor people. Loosely, it could be said that tagging will in consequence reduce the cost of income redistribution (since, with lower marginal tax rates, there is a smaller gap between social and private returns from work and therefore less loss of consumer's surplus due to redistribution-caused job switching). As a result, it is only natural that tagging increases the optimal transfers to poor people.

A. The rudimentary Mirrlees-Fair model

As implied by Mirrlees, there are no interesting easily solved algebraic examples of the optimal income tax with a continuum of abilities. There is no question that tagging, since it adds an additional degree of freedom, makes the problem still harder. Therefore, the example presented here is a much simplified version of the Mirrlees-Fair general case.

The example here is the most rudimentary model in which the optimal tax structure, both with and without tagging, is dictated by the tradeoffs between the deadweight loss due to taxes and subsidies and the gains of redistribution from rich to poor. Instead of a continuum of workers (as in Mirrlees), there are just two types: skilled and unskilled; instead of a continuum of output dependent upon labor input, there are just two types of jobs: difficult jobs (denoted by subscript D) and easy jobs (denoted by subscript E). Instead of a marginal condition describing the optimal tax reflecting continua of both labor input and worker types and the corresponding use of the calculus of variations, the optimum tax is characterized by a binding inequality constraint, which results from the discrete calculus corresponding to the discrete number of job types and worker types.

It is assumed that there are an equal number of skilled and unskilled workers. Skilled workers may work in either difficult or easy jobs, but unskilled workers may work only in easy jobs.[3] The output of a skilled worker in a difficult job is q_D, which is a constant

3 The model works out equivalently if unskilled workers can work in difficult jobs but have great distaste for the extra effort required.

Table 2. *Output of worker by type of worker by type of job*

Type of worker (percent of workforce)	Type of job	
	Difficult	Easy
Skilled (50%)	q_D	q_E
Unskilled (50%)	Not applicable	q_E

Note: $q_D > q_E$

independent of the number of workers in such jobs. Similarly, the output of both skilled and unskilled workers in easy jobs is q_E, which is also a constant independent of the number of workers in such jobs. These data are summarized in Table 2, which gives the technology of the model. Of course, output in difficult jobs exceeds output in easy jobs, so that $q_D > q_E$.

The economy is competitive, so that pretax, pretransfer pay in each job is the worker's marginal product in that job. The utility of each worker depends upon after-tax, after-transfer income and upon the nonpecuniary returns of his job. The utility functions can be written as a separable function of the pecuniary and the nonpecuniary returns. Let t_D denote the taxes paid by workers in difficult jobs (with income q_D), and let t_E denote transfers to workers in easy jobs (with income q_E). After-tax income in difficult jobs is $q_D - t_D$; after-transfer income in easy jobs is $q_E + t_E$. The utility of skilled workers in difficult jobs is $u(q_D - t_D) - \delta$, and the utility of both skilled and unskilled workers in easy jobs is $u(q_E + t_E)$. The parameter δ reflects the nonpecuniary distaste of workers for difficult jobs due to the greater effort necessary. Of course, $u' > 0$, $u'' < 0$. It is further assumed that $u(q_D) - \delta > u(q_E)$; otherwise, easy jobs dominate difficult jobs, so that, at the optimum, all workers (trivially) work in easy jobs without paying taxes or receiving transfers. The preceding data are summarized in Table 3.

In the absence of tagging, the Mirrlees-Fair optimal income tax, as applied to this model, is obtained by choosing a tax on income in difficult jobs t_D and a transfer to income in easy jobs t_E, subject to the

Table 3. *Utility of workers by type of worker by type of job, with taxes t_D on persons with pretax income q_D, and transfers t_E to persons with pretax income q_E*

| Type of worker | Type of job | |
(percent of workforce)	Difficult	Easy
Skilled (50%)	$u(q_D - t_D) - \delta$	$u(q_E + t_E)$
Unskilled (50%)	Not applicable	$u(q_E + t_E)$

Note: $u(q_D) - \delta > u(q_E)$

constraint that qualified workers will choose skilled or unskilled jobs depending upon which one yields greater utility (after taxes), and also subject to the constraint that taxes equal transfers. In mathematical form this becomes the maximization problem to choose t_D and t_E to maximize U,

$$(6) \quad U = \tfrac{1}{2} \max \{u(q_D - t_D) - \delta, u(q_E + t_E)\} \\ + \tfrac{1}{2} u(q_E + t_E)$$

subject to

$$(7a) \quad t_D = t_E \quad \text{if} \quad u(q_D - t_D) - \delta \geq u(q_E + t_E)$$
$$(7b) \quad t_E = 0 \quad \text{if} \quad u(q_D - t_D) - \delta < u(q_E + t_E)$$

It is convenient to denote optimal values with an asterisk. Thus the optimal value of U is U^*, of t is t^*, and of t_E is t_E^*.

The maximand (6) consists of the sum of the utilities of skilled and unskilled workers weighted by their respective fractions of the population. The utility of a skilled worker is $\max \{u(q_D - t_D) - \delta, u(q_E + t_E)\}$ since skilled workers are assumed to work in difficult jobs if $u(q_D - t_D) - \delta \geq u(q_E + t_E)$, and in easy jobs otherwise. Equations (7a) and (7b) jointly reflect the balanced budget constraint. If skilled workers work in difficult jobs, the tax collection per skilled worker is t_D. If tax collections equal transfers, $t_D = t_E$ (which is (7a)). However, if skilled workers work in easy jobs, they must receive the same transfer as unskilled workers. As a result, the condition that taxes equal transfers implies that $t_E = 0$, which is (7b).

Tagging does not occur in this maximization, since skilled and unskilled workers alike receive the same transfer t_E if they work in easy jobs.

Two equations, (8) and (9), characterize the optimal tax-*cum*-transfer rate t_D^* and t_E^* which maximize U:

(8) $t_D^* = t_E^*$

(9) $u(q_D - t_D^*) - \delta = u(q_E + t_E^*)$

Of course, (8) is the tax-equal-transfer balanced budget constraint. Equation (9) expresses the additional condition that, at the optimum, as much is redistributed from skilled to unskilled workers as possible, subject to the constraint that any greater redistribution would cause skilled workers to switch from difficult to easy jobs. (Any increase in t_D above t_D^*, or in t_E above t_E^*, results in a shift of all skilled workers into easy jobs.) As a result of this threatened shift, the deadweight loss due to a marginal increase in taxes or in transfers exceeds the returns from any redistributive gain.[4] Thus, our model, although rudimentary, has an optimal tax-*cum*-transfer schedule which reflects the tradeoffs of Mirrlees-Fair: the optimal tax/transfer policy being determined both by the gains from redistribution and the losses due to labor-supply shifts in response to changes in taxes and transfers.

B. Tagging introduced into rudimentary Mirrlees-Fair model

Now consider how tagging will alter the Mirrlees-Fair maximization and its solution. Suppose that a portion β of the unskilled workers can be identified (i.e., tagged) as unskilled and given a tax/transfer schedule different from that of other workers. In the altered model with tagging, let T_D denote the taxes paid by untagged workers in difficult jobs; let T_E denote transfers (perhaps negative) paid to untagged workers in easy jobs; and let τ denote the transfer to tagged workers (all of whom work in easy jobs). Table 4 compares the tax/transfer schedule of the earlier model without tagging and the tax schedule of the current model with tagging.

4 It also happens in this maximization that any further increase in taxes or in transfers at the margin causes such a large and discontinuous shift in the number of workers earning high incomes in difficult jobs that such an increase also decreases the revenues available for redistribution to unskilled workers.

Table 4. *Taxes on difficult jobs and transfers to easy jobs in models with and without tagging*

	Model without tagging	Model with tagging
Tax on difficult job	t_D	T_D
Transfer to easy job (workers untagged)	t_E	T_E
Transfer to easy job (workers tagged)	Not applicable	τ

Using Table 4, it is easy to construct Table 5, which gives the utility of workers by type of job after taxes and after transfers. Table 5 differs from Table 3 by addition of the bottom row, which represents the utility of tagged workers in easy jobs who receive the transfer τ.

Using the data in Table 5, it is easy to see that, with tagging, the optimum tax-*cum*-transfer policy is to choose the values (T_D, T_E, τ) that maximize U^{Tag}, where:

$$(10) \quad U^{Tag} = \tfrac{1}{2} \max \{u(q_D - T_D) - \delta, u(q_E + T_E)\}$$
$$+ \tfrac{1}{2}(1 - \beta)u(q_E + T_E) + \tfrac{1}{2}\beta u(q_E + \tau)$$

subject to the balanced budget constraints (11a) and (11b):

$$(11a) \quad T_D = (1 - \beta)T_E + \beta\tau \quad \text{if} \quad u(q_D - T_D) - \delta$$
$$\geq u(q_E + T_E)$$
$$(11b) \quad (2 - \beta)T_E + \beta\tau = 0 \quad \text{if} \quad u(q_D - T_D) - \delta$$
$$< u(q_E + T_E)$$

Again, denote the optimum values with an asterisk: T_D^*, T_E^*, τ^*, and U^{Tag*}.

The maximand U^{Tag} is the sum of the utility of all three types of workers – skilled, untagged unskilled, and tagged unskilled – weighted by their respective fractions of the population. The utility of skilled workers is $u(q_D - T_D) - \delta$ or $u(q_E + T_E)$, dependent upon whether they choose difficult or easy jobs. Equations (11a) and (11b) are the tax-equal-transfer, balanced-budget constraints. The respective equation applies accordingly as skilled workers are in difficult or in easy jobs.

Table 5. *Utility of worker by type of worker by type of job with tagging; untagged workers pay taxes T_D in difficult jobs and receive transfers T_E in unskilled jobs; tagged workers receive a transfer τ in unskilled jobs*

Type of worker (fraction of workforce)	Type of job	
	Difficult	Easy
Skilled (Untagged) (½)	$u(q_D - T_D) - \delta$	$u(q_E + T_E)$
Unskilled (Untagged) $((1 - \beta)/2)$	Not applicable	$u(q_E + T_E)$
Unskilled (Tagged) $(\beta/2)$	Not applicable	$u(q_E + \tau)$

In the Appendix, it is shown that with $u(q_D) - \delta > u(q_E)$, for $0 < \beta \leq 1$, the optimal transfer to tagged workers τ^* exceeds the optimal transfer to untagged unskilled workers t_E^* in the model without tagging. With $\beta = 1$, complete equality of income is attained at the optimum. In this precise sense, tagging increases the optimum transfers to those who are identified as poor and given special tax treatment.

The difference between the tagging and the nontagging optimization is clear: with tagging, for a given increased subsidy to tagged people, there is a smaller decline in the income differential between difficult and easy work, since T_E need not shift, and there is therefore a smaller tendency for workers to shift from difficult to easy jobs with a given redistribution of income. As a result, optimal transfers to tagged workers are greater with tagging than in its absence.

An outline of the proof, which is given in the Appendix, illustrates the application of this logic more particularly. The proof shows that, at the optimum, the rate of taxation of workers in difficult jobs and the rate of transfer to untagged workers in easy jobs is taken up to the point that any further increase in either of those two rates will induce skilled workers to shift into easy jobs. This is reflected by the optimization condition (12), which is exactly analogous to the similar optimization condition (9) in the untagged case:

$$(12) \quad u(q_D - T_D^*) - \delta = u(q_E + T_E^*)$$

It is then shown by contradiction that τ^* (the optimal transfer to tagged workers) exceeds T_E^* (the optimal transfer to unskilled untagged workers). Suppose the contrary (i.e., $\tau^* \leq T_E^*$). In that case, a marginal decrease in T_E and a marginal increase in equal dollar amount in τ can cause no decrease in utility, while it allows some additional redistribution to be made from skilled workers in difficult jobs to other workers without inducing any skilled workers to switch from difficult into easy jobs. Since total utility U^{Tag} is sure to be increased by at least one of these two changes and not decreased by the other, the optimality of τ^* and T_E^* is contradicted. At the optimum, therefore, τ^* must be greater than T_E^*.

Knowing that $\tau^* > T_E^*$, as has been shown, knowing that T_D^* and T_E^* satisfy (12), and knowing that t_D^* and t_E^* satisfy the similar condition (9), $u(q_D - t_D^*) - \delta = u(q_E + t_E^*)$, the budget constraints can be used to show that $\tau^* > t_E^*$.

IV. Generalized problem

In the example in the last section, there was no opportunity for people to change the characteristics by which they were tagged. Age, race, and sex are real life examples of such characteristics. However, there are also redistribution programs in which people, by some effort or with some loss of utility, may alter their characteristics, thereby becoming members of a tagged group. The most commonly cited example of this concerns families who allegedly have separated in order to obtain payments under the Aid to Dependent Children program (see Daniel Moynihan).

To consider the case more generally, in which group membership is endogenous, this section presents a general model. It then becomes an empirical (rather than a theoretical) question to determine what amount of tagging (and quite possibly the answer is none) will maximize aggregate utility U. There is no major theorem in general, unless it is the falsity of the proposition to which the previous section gave a counterexample, that a uniform negative income tax is always superior to a welfare system that gives special aid to people with special problems or characteristics.

In general, we may assume the goal is to choose functions $t_\gamma(y_\gamma)$ to maximize

$$(13) \quad U = \int u_x f(x) \, dx$$

where $f(x)$ denotes the distribution of people of type x, and where the utility of such a person depends on his after-tax income, his characteristics, and the group to which he belongs γ, or

$$(14) \quad u_x = u(y - t, x, \gamma)$$

In the real world, of course, tagging is not costless, one of the major complaints against the current welfare system being its cost of administration. Let Γ be the grouping of people into various subgroups of the population, and let $c(\Gamma)$ be the administrative cost of such tagging.

U is maximized subject to two constraints, the first being that taxes equal transfers plus administrative costs, or

$$(15) \quad \int_x t_\gamma(y(x), \gamma(x)) f(x) \, dx + c(\Gamma) = 0$$

where $\gamma(x)$ is the group to which an individual of type x belongs, and the second being that an individual of type x chooses his labor input and the group to which he belongs to maximize

$$(16) \quad u[w(x, \gamma)L(x, \gamma) - t_\gamma(w(x, \gamma)L(x, \gamma)), L(x,\gamma), x, \gamma]$$

where $w(x, \gamma)$ is the wage of a person of characteristic x belonging to group γ, and $L(x, \gamma)$ is the labor input.

In sum, this is the generalization of Mirrlees' (and Fair's) problem to taxation with tagging. I have taken the trouble to specify this general problem since it is important to note the potential endogeneity of the tagged characteristics and of administrative costs.

V. Cost-benefit evaluation of manpower programs and tagging

Another type of program in which tagging is important is manpower training programs. Typically, such programs in the United States have aimed at improving the skills of the disadvantaged and the temporarily unemployed. Because of formal eligibility requirements, and also because of self-selectivity of the trainees, people in special need are identified (or tagged) by such programs.

There has been an intensive effort in the United States to evaluate the benefits and costs of such programs, so much so that there have been extensive "reviews of the reviews" (see David O'Neill). The studies have typically (but with some exceptions) found that the benefits of manpower training programs, as conventionally accounted, have been less than the costs. But because of the value of tagging done by such programs, a benefit-cost ratio of less than unity is not sufficient reason for their curtailment.

This last point can be made formally in terms of the tagging models in Sections III and IV. A manpower program could be introduced into the model in Section III by assuming that, at a given cost per worker, an unskilled worker who is previously untagged can be made into a skilled worker. The costs of such a program, as usually accounted, are its costs of operation plus the wages foregone by workers while engaged in training. The cost of operation becomes an additional term in the balanced budget constraint (analogous to the term $c(\Gamma)$ in (15)). The benefits from the program are the increase in the pretax, pretransfer wages of the worker subsequent to training. It is easy to construct an example in which the benefits (thus accounted) are less than the costs (thus accounted), yet U^{Tag} is greater with the program than in its absence, because the program tags unskilled workers and makes income redistribution possible with relatively little distortion to the incentive structure.

An unrigorous calculation using consumer's surplus logic shows that the tagging benefits of manpower programs may be substantial. Consider two subgroups of the population, both of which are young and both of which have low current incomes. One group is skilled but has low current income because it is building up human capital; the other group is unskilled and has low current income for that reason; it also has low permanent income.

Let there be a manpower training program. At a cost of c dollars, the permanent income of a young unskilled worker can be raised by

$1. The costs of this program (as usually accounted) are c dollars, and its benefits are $1. Considering consumer's surplus and assuming that there is a deadweight loss of λ per dollar due to taxes to pay for the program, the cost of the program, inclusive of deadweight loss, is $c(1 + \lambda)$.

Now compare the advantages of this training program to a negative income tax that gives lump sum transfers to all young workers, whether skilled or unskilled. Let unskilled workers be a fraction θ of the total population. To redistribute $1 to an unskilled young worker, a total of $1/\theta$ dollars must be redistributed to all young people.

Which scheme – the manpower training program or the negative income tax – is the cheaper way of redistributing $1 to unskilled workers? The cost, inclusive of deadweight loss of the manpower program, is $c(1 + \lambda)$. The cost, inclusive of deadweight loss of the negative income tax, is the deadweight loss on $1/\theta$ dollars, plus the $1 redistributed, or $\lambda/\theta + 1$. Which scheme is cheaper depends upon whether $c(1 + \lambda)$ is greater or less than $(\lambda/\theta + 1)$.

Let λ be .05 and let θ be .1, numbers which are not unrepresentative of reasonable parameters for deadweight loss due to income taxation and the fraction of the population eligible for a typical manpower training program such as the Job Corps. If the benefit-cost ratio of the manpower program $(1/c)$ is less than .7, the negative income tax is the cheaper method of redistribution; if the benefit-cost ratio is greater than .7, the manpower program is preferable.

VI. Summary and conclusions

This paper has identified the important tradeoffs in the design of institutions to redistribute income. Some types of programs, either by their eligibility requirements or by the self-selection of the beneficiaries, identify (tag) people who are in special need. With tagging, taxpayers (as opposed to beneficiaries) are denied the benefit of the transfer, so that in effect a *lump sum* transfer is made to tagged people.

In contrast, with a negative income tax, a grant is made to all taxpayers and this grant must be recovered to achieve the same net revenue. This recovery results in high marginal tax rates, whose disincentive effects are the major disadvantage of a negative income tax. This disadvantage, however, must be weighed against the disadvantages of tagging, which are the perverse incentives to people to be identified as needy (to be tagged), the inequity of such a system, and its cost of administration.

The problem of the optimal redistributional system, both with and without tagging, has been set up in the framework of the Mirrlees-Fair optimal income tax. It was shown in a special example that if a portion of the poor population could be identified (costlessly, in this example), total welfare U could be raised by giving increased subsidies to the tagged poor.

Finally, the consequences of tagging for manpower programs were discussed. Since tagging is a benefit of most manpower programs, benefit-cost ratios need not exceed unity to justify their existence. In fact, an example showed that benefit/cost ratios could be significantly less than one (.7 in this example), and a manpower program might still be preferable to a negative income tax as a method of income redistribution.

Appendix

Theorem 1: *Using the definitions of τ^* and t_E^* in Section III, and also the models in that section, if $u(q_D) - \delta > u(q_E)$ and $0 < \beta \leq 1, \tau^* > t_E^*$.*

Proof. The proof proceeds by five propositions. Propositions 1 and 2 make variational arguments which show that at the maximum as much must be redistributed from skilled workers as possible without inducing them to switch into easy jobs. This yields the condition:

$$(A1) \quad u(q_D - T_D^*) - \delta = u(q_E + T_E^*)$$

It is similarly true without tagging that

$$(A2) \quad u(q_D - t_D^*) - \delta = u(q_E + t_E^*)$$

From (A1) and (A2) it can be easily shown (Proposition 3) that if $T_D^* > t_D^*$, $T_E^* < t_E^*$ (and vice versa).

Proposition 4 then shows that $\tau^* \geq t_E^*$. There are two cases. In one case, $T_D^* < t_D^*$. If $T_D^* < t_D^*$, by Proposition 3, $T_E^* > t_E^*$. Suppose $t_E^* \geq \tau^*$. A variational argument shows that this cannot be a maximum, for a decrease in T_E^* and an increase in τ^* can increase U^{Tag}. In the other case, $T_D^* \geq t_D^*$. But if $T_D^* \geq t_D^*$, by Proposition 3, $T_E^* \leq t_E^*$. It follows from the balanced budget constraints that if T_E^* is smaller than t_E^*, but also, T_D^* is larger than t_D^*, that τ^* must be larger than t_E^*. As a result, in both Case I and Case II, $\tau^* \geq t_E^*$. Proposition 5 shows that the inequality is strict.

Proposition 1. $u(q_D - T_D^*) - \delta \geq u(q_E + T_E^*)$

Proof. Suppose otherwise. Then,

(A3) $U^{Tag^*} = \frac{1}{2}\{(2 - \beta)u(q_E + T_E^*)$
$$+ \beta u(q_E + \tau^*)\} \leq u(q_E)$$

by the concavity of u and the constraint (11b) that $(2 - \beta)T_E^* = -\beta\tau^*$. Since $u(q_D) - \delta > u(q_E)$ by assumption,

(A4) $u(q_E) < \frac{1}{2}\{u(q_D) - \delta + u(q_E)\}$

Since $T_D = T_E = \tau = 0$ is a feasible tax/transfer vector (satisfying budget constraint (11)), and with

(A5) $U^{Tag} = \frac{1}{2}\{u(q_D) - \delta + u(q_E)\}$

the optimality of U^{Tag^*} is contradicted by (A3), (A4), and (A5). By this contradiction,

(A6) $u(q_D - T_D^*) - \delta \geq u(q_E + T_E^*)$

Proposition 2.

(A7) $u(q_D - T_D^*) - \delta = u(q_E + T_E^*)$

Proof. Suppose that $u(q_D - T_D^*) - \delta > u(q_E + T_E^*)$. A variational argument shows that (T_D^*, T_E^*, τ^*) is not optimal.

Let $T_D' = T_D^* + \epsilon$
$\quad\quad T_E' = T_E^* + \epsilon/(1 - \beta)$

(A8) $\quad U^{Tag}(T'_D, T'_E, \tau^*) = U^{Tag}(T^*_D, T^*_E, \tau^*)$
$$+ \epsilon/2[-u'(q_D - T^*_D) + u'(q_E + T^*_E)] + o^2(\epsilon)$$

where $o^2(\epsilon)$ is an expression with $\lim_{\epsilon \to 0} o^2(\epsilon)/\epsilon^2 = 0$. But since $u(q_D - T^*_D) - \delta > u(q_E + T^*_E)$ by assumption,

(A9) $\quad u'(q_D - T^*_D) < u'(q_E + T^*_E)$

by the concavity of u.

Therefore, by (A8), $U^{Tag}(T'_D, T'_E, \tau^*) > U^{Tag}(T^*_D, T^*_E, \tau^*)$ for ϵ sufficiently small, which contradicts the optimality of (T^*_D, T^*_E, τ^*). Therefore, $u(q_D - T^*_D) - \delta \leq u(q_E + T^*_E)$.

By Proposition 1, $u(q_D - T^*_D) - \delta \geq u(q_E + T^*_E)$. Therefore,

(A10) $\quad u(q_D - T^*_D) - \delta = u(q_E + T^*_E)$

Proposition 3. $T^*_D > t^*_D$ *if and only if* $T^*_E < t^*_E$.

Proof. Suppose $T^*_D > t^*_D$. By Proposition 2

(A11) $\quad u(q_D - T^*_D) - \delta = u(q_E + T^*_E)$

By similar logic,

(A12) $\quad u(q_D - t^*_D) - \delta = u(q_E + t^*_E)$

If $T^*_D > t^*_D$, then

(A13) $\quad u(q_D - T^*_D) < u(q_D - t^*_D)$

whence

(A14)
$$\begin{aligned} &u(q_E + T^*_E) \\ = &\; u(q_D - T^*_D) - \delta < u(q_D - t^*_D) - \delta \\ = &\; u(q_E + t^*_E) \end{aligned}$$

(A15) $\quad T^*_E < t^*_E$

Similarly, if $T^*_D < t^*_D$, $T^*_E > t^*_E$

Proposition 4. $\tau^* \geq t_E^*$.

Proof. Suppose

(A16) $\tau^* < t_E^*$

It will be shown that the optimality of τ^* or of t_E^* is contradicted. Two cases will be analyzed:

Case I: $T_D^* < t_D^*$
Case II: $T_D^* \geq t_D^*$

Case I: By Proposition 3, if $T_D^* < t_D^*$,

(A17) $T_E^* > t_E^*$

But then

(A18) $U^{Tag}(T_D^*, T_E^* - \epsilon, \tau^* + (1 - \beta)/\beta\epsilon) = U^{Tag}(T_D^*, T_E^*, \tau^*)$

$$- (1 - \beta)\epsilon/2u'(q_E + T_E^*) + \beta\frac{1 - \beta}{\beta}\epsilon/2u'(q_E + \tau^*) + o^2(\epsilon)$$

which last equation (A18) for sufficiently small ϵ

(A19) $> U^{Tag}(T_D^*, T_E^*, \tau^*)$

since $u'(q_E + T_E^*) < u'(q_E + t_E^*) < u'(q_E + \tau^*)$ by the concavity of u and by both the inequality (A17), ($T_E^* > t_E^*$), and the supposition (A16), ($t_E^* > \tau^*$). The inequality (A19) contradicts the optimality of (T_D^*, T_E^*, τ^*). Therefore, if $T_D^* < t_D^*, \tau^* \geq t_E^*$.

Case II: $T_D^* \geq t_D^*$.

Suppose again

(A20) $\tau^* < t_E^*$

We will show a contradiction. By Proposition 3, if $T_D^* \geq t_D^*$,

(A21) $T_E^* \leq t_E^*$

By inequality (A21), $(T_E^* \leq t_E^*)$, the budget constraint (7a), $(t_D^* = t_E^*)$, and inequality (A20), $(\tau^* < t_E^*)$,

(A22) $T_D^* \geq t_D^* = t_E^* > (1 - \beta)T_E^* + \beta\tau^*$

which contradicts the budget constraint (11a), which states:

(A23) $T_D^* = (1 - \beta)T_E^* + \beta\tau^*$

Hence, if $T_D^* \geq t_D^*$, $\tau^* \geq t_E^*$.
    Combining Cases I and II, it has been shown that $\tau^* \geq t_E^*$.

Proposition 5. $\tau^* > t_E^*$.

Proof. It remains to show that $\tau^* \neq t_E^*$. Suppose the contrary, that $\tau^* = t_E^*$. A contradiction will be demonstrated. By Proposition 3 at the optimum

(A24) $u(q_D - T_D^*) - \delta = u(q_E + T_E^*)$

and similarly,

(A25) $u(q_D - t_D^*) - \delta = u(q_E + t_E^*)$

The optimum (T_D^*, T_E^*, τ^*) and (t_D^*, t_E^*) must also satisfy the budget constraints (7a) and (11a):

(A26) $T_D^* = (1 - \beta)T_E^* + \beta\tau^*$

(A27) $t_D^* = t_E^*$

Add to the system (A24) to (A27) the assumption (A28):

(A28) $\tau^* = t_E^*$

An optimum with $\tau^* = t_E^*$ must satisfy the five relations (A24) to (A28). These five equations constitute a system of five equations in the five variables $(T_D^*, T_E^*, \tau^*, t_D^*, t_E^*)$, with unique solution with the property

$$T_D^* = T_E^* = \tau^* = t_D^* = t_E^*$$

Let

(A29) $T_D' = T_D^* + 2\epsilon_1$

(A30) $T_E' = T_E^* - 2\epsilon_2$

(A31) $\tau' = \tau^* + \dfrac{1 - \beta}{\beta} 2\epsilon_2 + \dfrac{1}{\beta} 2\epsilon_1$

with

(A32) $\epsilon_1 < \dfrac{u'(q_D - T_D^*)}{u'(q_E + T_E^*)} \epsilon_2$

Then,

(A33) $U^{Tag}(T_D', T_E', \tau') = U^{Tag}(T_D^*, T_E^*, \tau^*) - \epsilon_1 u'(q_D - T_D^*)$

$\qquad - (1 - \beta)\epsilon_2 u'(q_E + T_E^*) + \beta \dfrac{\epsilon_1}{\beta} u'(q_E + \tau^*)$

$\qquad + \beta \dfrac{1 - \beta}{\beta} \epsilon_2 u'(q_E + \tau^*) + o^2(\epsilon_1) + o^2(\epsilon_2)$

Since $\tau^* = T_E^*$, for (ϵ_1, ϵ_2) sufficiently small $U^{Tag}(T_D', T_E', \tau') > U^{Tag}(T_D^*, T_E^*, \tau^*)$, which contradicts the optimality of (T_D^*, T_E^*, τ^*). Hence, $\tau^* \neq t_E^*$. And, using Proposition 4, $\tau^* > t_E^*$.

References

R. C. Fair, "The Optimal Distribution of Income," *Quart. J. Econ.*, Nov. 1971, *85*, 557–79.

J. A. Mirrlees, "An Exploration in the Optimal Theory of Income Taxation," *Rev. Econ. Stud.*, Apr. 1971, *38*, 175–208.

D. P. Moynihan, "The Negro Family: The Case for National Action," in L. Rainwater and W. L. Yancey, eds., *The Moynihan Report and the Politics of Controversy*, Cambridge, Mass. 1967.

D. M. O'Neill, "The Federal Government and Manpower: A Critical Look at the MDTA-Institutional and Job Corps Programs," American Enterprise Institute for Policy Research, 1973.

New York Times, Aug. 9, 1969; Apr. 21, 1970; July 23, 1971.

U.S. Council of Economic Advisers, *Economic Report of the President,* Washington D.C., 1974.

5

A theory of social custom, of which unemployment may be one consequence

This paper examines adherence to social customs. Models of social customs are found to be inherently multi-equilibrial. It is found that social customs which are disadvantageous to the individual may nevertheless persist without erosion, if individuals are sanctioned by loss of reputation for disobedience of the custom. One example of such a social custom is the persistence of a fair (rather than a market-clearing) wage. In this fashion, involuntary unemployment is explained.

I. Introduction

There are many social customs whose disobedience under the right circumstances is of pecuniary advantage to the person who disobeys.[1] Furthermore, if the sin of not following a social custom is considered less serious if disobedience is more common, in all likelihood the values responsible for the observance of a social custom are less likely to be passed on from one generation to the next the greater is the disobedience. It might be expected, in consequence, that even in a state of the world in which the beliefs underlying a social custom are universally accepted, some persons with unusual tastes will be attracted by the pecuniary gain from breaking it; this breaking of the social custom will, at least to some extent, undermine the beliefs responsible for its observance; and this undermining of belief will in turn provoke

The author would like to thank Kenneth Arrow, William Brainard, Franklin Fisher, Jerry Green, Sanford Grossman, Ross Milbourne, Hajime Miyazaki, Max Steuer, Peter Tinsley, James Tobin, Laurence Weiss, Janet Yellen, and two anonymous referees for valuable comments. The first drafts of this paper were written while the author was Visiting Research Economist in the Special Studies Section, Division of Research and Statistics, Board of Governors of the Federal Reserve System. He would like to thank the Federal Reserve for generous financial support while writing this paper.

1 A social custom is an act whose utility to the agent performing it in some way depends on the beliefs or actions of other members of the community. These two types of endogenous utility are represented here by equations (1), (2), and (3).

more disobedience, etc. – in such a sequence of increasing disobedience and erosion of belief that in the long run the social custom disappears. This paper explains why such a sequence need not occur – despite pecuniary advantage from disobeying a social custom, and despite disobedience undermining belief in the social code responsible for its observance. Accordingly, it is explained why social customs that are costly for the individual to follow persist nevertheless. The binding force that causes this persistence, as will be explained at considerable length, is the social sanction imposed by loss of reputation from breaking the custom.

The question regarding the relation between the profit motive and social customs is not new to economists, being implicit in the writings of Becker [1957, 1965, 1968, 1973, 1974] on discrimination and other social customs, and quite explicit in Arrow's essay [1972] on discrimination. According to that essay, neoclassical theory is unsatisfactory in explaining racial discrimination because it fails to explain why entrepreneurs who could make profits by hiring labor cheaply from the discriminated-against group fail to do so. Arrow puts the matter quite colorfully:

> Sherlock Holmes, a man much concerned with the formulation of hypotheses for the explanation of empirical behavior, once asked about the barking of a dog at night. The local police inspector, mystified as usual, noted that the dog had not barked at night. Holmes dryly noted that the silence was precisely the problem. Have we some dog whose silence should be remarked? Yes; those vast forces of greed and aggressiveness that we are assured and assure students are the mainsprings of economic activity in a private enterprise economy; not the best, but the strongest motives of humanity, as Marshall had said ... [1972, p. 90].

Arrow's own answer to his question is not clear in the context of his whole essay, which contains, among other things, the famous "signaling" explanation for black/white wage differentials. In the narrow context, however, of the possibility of group enforcement of discrimination, Arrow [1972, p. 99] says that "the argument would have to be that the discriminatory tastes ... are themselves the mechanism by which discrimination profitable to the whites is carried out." At least in the context of this remark, Arrow and Becker are in complete accord, since discriminatory tastes are totally responsible for discrimination in the Becker model.

The present essay begins where Becker and Arrow have left off. Even if at any point in time discriminatory tastes can cause discrimination (regarding which possibility Arrow expresses some important doubts), the question remains why over the longer run the social values responsible for discrimination are not increasingly eroded by nonobservance of social custom caused by pecuniary gain. To be more explicit, with the Becker model of discrimination any individual with discriminatory tastes pays for those tastes, because he gives up pecuniary consumption insofar as he (implicitly) purchases "discriminatory services." Disobedience due to the pecuniary advantage to nondiscrimination will cause each subsequent generation to have fewer persons with tastes for discrimination, provided that the children's generation has greater or lesser utility for observance of a social custom, accordingly, as obedience to social custom exceeds or falls short of belief in the social values for its observance. Given this last hypothesis regarding the intergenerational formation of tastes, Arrow's forces of greed and aggressiveness will accomplish in the long run what they failed to do in the short run. They will have eliminated discrimination; the dog will have barked, although perhaps fairly late in the night.

In the model that is presented below, a custom, once established, will persist, provided that disobedience of the custom results in sufficient loss of reputation, and provided that the cost of disobedience is sufficiently high. For this reason, with a given set of social values, there are two stable equilibria. In one of these equilibria the custom is obeyed, and the values underlying the custom are widely subscribed to by members of the community. In the other equilibrium the custom has disappeared, no one believes in the values underlying it, and it is not obeyed. As a result, if the major features of the model accurately reproduce the major features of reality, Becker's marginal analysis of customs, while correct (at the margin), also misses the important point. Marginal methods are appropriate for comparative static analysis of a single equilibrium. However, with more than one equilibrium, marginal analysis of a single equilibrium fails to analyze the causes for movement from one equilibrium to another. Furthermore, there are multiple equilibria in the sense that many different customs, once established, could be followed in equilibrium. Indeed, such multiplicity is the essence of social custom: it is inherent in the adage, "When in Rome, do as the Romans do."

The existence of custom-preserving equilibria is, we claim, the key to another problem of economic theorists. It has been stated recently (by Robert Hall [1975], Edmund Phelps [1972], and James Tobin [1972], to name three specific examples) that economists do not yet have a satisfactory theory of involuntary unemployment. By this statement it is meant that economists have been unable to use utility analysis to produce models in which wages and prices do not adjust so that all markets, of which the labor market is no exception, clear. Except in the most bizarre circumstances, if such markets do not clear, there cannot be a Nash equilibrium; for two traders, one a buyer and the other a seller, would be willing to trade at other than the nonmarket-clearing price. Thus, by its nature standard economic analysis all but precludes *involuntary* unemployment.

The social customs model that is presented below, however, can break the preceding chain of logic, for a social custom may be obeyed even though it is to everyone's individual economic disadvantage to obey it. A social custom that proscribes the competitive actions necessary to achieve a market-clearing price may be obeyed by utility-maximizing agents fearful of the consequences of disobeying the custom.[2] In the model below, transactions between employees and employers have a traditional code of behavior that precludes trades at the market-clearing prices. Such a code, it is shown in the next three sections, can be consistent with equilibrium either if persons are reluctant to lose reputation by breaking it or if their belief in it is sufficiently strong. As long as social custom is observed, therefore, unemployment will occur. In our model, in both the long run and the short run, there are equilibria in which this social custom is, in fact, observed.

It is not to be supposed that the code of behavior in this example is considered realistic. On the contrary, it is chosen for its simplicity, not for its realism. Rather, it is meant to illustrate that nonindividualistic-maximizing behavior may result in equilibria that are qualitatively different from those obtained from individualistic-maximizing behavior; and this qualitative difference goes as far as the possibility of nonmarket clearance. We do believe, however, that some expanded version of our model, with a far more complex (per-

---

2 Earlier papers on sanctions are Akerlof [1976] and Akerlof and Soskice [1976]. This paper answers the difficulty in the earlier papers that small coalitions could break the sanctions equilibrium.

haps it should be said, "realistic") description of the community's code of market behavior, including some codes regarding "fair" wages, will result in unemployment which is similar to the unemployment obtained in our model.

To illustrate such a situation that is more complex than our model and also more realistic, suppose the custom prohibits an employer from hiring labor at a reduced money wage. There may be unemployed labor willing to work at such a money wage (if there is involuntary unemployment), but the employer cannot profitably hire such labor because his current work force will not train the new workers (even though the training cost of new workers is zero if the existing work force cooperates with on-the-job training). Yet each laborer refuses to aid in the training because by doing so he would suffer a loss of reputation, according to the norms of his society, if he should cooperate with the employer in engaging in the prohibited action. Note: there are unemployed persons willing to work at the money wage currently paid by employers and for even less. Training costs are at the margin zero (although not for the full work force). Nevertheless, no parties will cooperate to eliminate the gap in the supply and demand for labor.

Admittedly, the preceding illustration is quite mundane; yet in contrast to such a mundane story, economic theorists have developed far more complex and, we should add, elegant theories of unemployment. We refer especially to search theory and to implicit contract theory.[3] Yet these other theories have theoretical and empirical difficulties. A more mundane picture of unemployment, while perhaps less elegant theoretically, can easily be more realistic, its very mundaneness being a recommendation of its realism.

II. General differences between our model and the usual Walrasian models with individualistic utility

A. Existence of a code of behavior

The first assumption that is not made in the standard economic model is the existence of a code of honor or a code of behavior in the relevant trading community, with a fraction of the population (denoted μ) subscribing to this code of behavior. The value of μ is not necessarily

3 See Azariadis [1975], Baily [1974], and Phelps et al. [1970].

zero or unity. A large share of cultural anthropology is devoted to the description of such codes of behavior of different societies.[4]

B. Dependence of utility on reputation

The second major assumption of the model, which differentiates it from an example of the usual Arrow-Debreu economy, concerns the role of reputation in preferences. In particular, it is assumed that persons care about their reputations in their respective communities in addition to caring about their consumption of goods and services and, for believers in the community's code of honor, in addition to caring about the agreement of their actions with that code. Anthropological studies abound with evidence that persons care deeply about their reputations in their communities.[5] According to our model, persons want to be "rich *and famous*" – the *and-famous* part of the expression not being redundant.

In sum, an individual's utility depends upon four arguments plus his own personal tastes, so that

(1) $U = U(G, R, A, d^C, \epsilon),$

where

G is a vector representing his consumption of material goods and services;

R represents his reputation in the community;

A is a dummy variable representing his obedience or disobedience of the community's code of behavior;

---

4 For example, see Kroeber [1923] and Benedict [1961].

5 To give three illustrations of writings about reputation and its role in causing individual actions, consider the village women in France as described by F. G. Bailey [1971], who outside their own homes are seen scurrying from place to place, holding up their aprons so as to avoid the impression of having *mauvaise langue* (or of passing malicious gossip), as women in small villages are allegedly wont to do; or consider, to change sexes and continents, the Kwakiutl Indian chiefs who at banquets attempt to simulate the greatest indifference by causing the greatest amount of wealth (in the form of blankets) to be literally turned to smoke (Benedict [1961]); or, for a third example, consider the conspicuous consumption of early Twentieth Century Americans as recorded by Thorstein Veblen [1899].

d^C is a dummy variable representing his belief or disbelief in this code of behavior; and

ϵ represents his personal tastes.

All five variables in (1) are necessary to represent the historical problem that was posed in the introduction. That question was whether unusual personal tastes (ϵ) would not cause there to be some believers in the code who disobey it, so that in the next generation the number of persons who are believers in the code (d^C = belief in the code), which is influenced by the number of persons who obey it, will be smaller; in the long run utility will be maximized only as a function of goods and services and ϵ. According to this paper, the appearance of reputation (R) in the utility function may cause a stable equilibrium with a stable number of believers in the code and of persons who obey that code.[6] How reputation is established, as is next described, is important to that theory.

C. Reputation function

The reputation of an individual depends on his obedience of the code of behavior of the community and also on the portion of the population μ who believe in that code. The larger the number of believers, the more reputation is lost by disobedience of the code.

Reputation can therefore be written as a function of μ and A:

(2) $R = R(A, \mu).$

Reputation formation (2), we feel, gives a good representation of the findings of anthropological studies, in which those who disobey the norms of most communities are in some way or other ostracized from that community.

D. Utility formation function

This last major way in which our model differs from an example of an Arrow-Debreu economy models the utility formation described in the introduction.

6 There may also be a stable equilibrium if persons who believe in the code have such strong beliefs that no believer in the code is willing to disobey it for pecuniary advantage. See Proposition II below.

The exact form of the assumption is derived not from any desire for realism, but from a desire for simplicity. It is the object of this paper to "try this assumption on for size," so to speak, to test the agreement (or lack thereof) between theory with this kind of utility formation and the nonindividualistic arguments to utility already described with the theory of the standard individualistic models with exogenous preferences.

According to this assumption, persons who disobey the code of honor of a community undermine belief in that code of honor. If there are fewer persons obeying the code of honor in the current generation than there are believers, there will be fewer believers in the next generation, and vice versa, so that

$$(3) \quad \dot{\mu} = g(\mu, x),$$

where μ is (as already mentioned) the fraction of the population that believes in the code and x is the fraction of the population that obeys it. If $\mu > x$, g is negative; if $\mu < x$, g is positive.

E. Summary

This concludes the general description of the four ways in which our model differs from the usual model of general equilibrium. The rest of the model is constructed to parallel the standard Walrasian model of pure exchange insofar as that is possible. The model is analyzable in terms of a short run and a long run. In the short run the fraction μ who believe in the society's code of honor is fixed. This fraction μ is a major determinant of the loss of reputation from disobeying the code of honor as reflected in equation (2); it also represents the fraction of the population that loses utility directly from disobedience of the code (as reflected in the presence of the variable d^C in equation (1) for a fraction μ of the population). With utility functions that are fixed with a given value of μ and with the operation of markets otherwise described by Walrasian exchange, consider the economy's equilibrium. By definition, in an equilibrium neither is it mutually advantageous for two parties to renege on any previously agreed trades with other agents and trade further with each other; nor is it mutually advantageous for a single party to renege on a trade to which he has agreed. In some cases, the code of honor of the community prevents trades that would occur in the absence of that code because the individuals involved in the trades believe in the code and do not wish to disobey it. Alternatively, individuals who do not believe in the code may nevertheless refrain from making trades that they consider economically advantageous because of the consequences of loss of reputation among the rest of the community. Thus, the short-run equilibrium may follow the Walrasian model up to a point; but there is the additional amendment that social customs may act as a constraint on economic activity, preventing trades that would occur in the absence of such a code.

Not only may the short run have equilibria in which the code acts as at least a partial constraint on some activity, but also the long run may have such equilibria, even if disobedience of the code tends to undermine beliefs in its underlying values (as suggested by equation (3)). In one case, even though disobedience of the code results in fewer believers in its underlying values, it may have no effect on the obedience of the code, since nonbelievers may also obey the code due to fear of loss of reputation among the believers in the rest of the community. Thus, the presence of a small number of disbelievers does not necessarily set in motion a process that cumulatively undermines the system's social values. In another case, belief in the custom may be so strong that increased disbelief in the code in no way affects the obedience of the code by believers. In that case, again, there is a long-run equilibrium in which the code will be obeyed.

In two senses the preceding analysis has multiple equilibria. First, with a given code there may be two equilibria; in one of these almost everyone believes the code, and almost everyone obeys it; in the other equilibrium almost no one believes the code, and almost no one obeys it. In this sense there are two equilibria with a given code of behavior. Additionally, however, the system can be thought to have many equilibria, since there may be a whole range of social codes that are at least partially observed in equilibrium. Since this range of social customs is consistent with equilibrium, the economy can be considered to have multiple equilibria.

An example is given in Section III and is analyzed in Sections IV, V, and VI that illustrates the possibility of a social custom that could be binding in the long run, even though individuals who cared neither about the social custom nor about their own reputations could gain by breaking it. According to this example, social custom dictates that capital must be traded for labor at a fixed ratio. Since this ratio dictates the terms of trade of capital for labor in equilibrium for a whole range of values, the example illustrates the multiplicity of equilibria in the second sense that a whole range of social customs may be observed in long-run equilibrium.

III. The particular model

A. Particularizations

The previous section described ways in which utility was nonindividualistic in our model, in contrast to the usual general equilibrium theory. Assumptions I to VI are particularizations; they particularize, for the sake of example, the initial endowments of agents, the utility functions of agents with given tastes, the code of behavior, the reputation function, the distribution of agents with given tastes, and the utility formation function. Assumptions VII to IX then describe market structure. The market structure described will yield a pure Arrow-Debreu economy in the absence of the nonindividualistic aspects of utility that have been described.

Assumption I: Initial endowments. The agents in the economy can be divided into two groups according to their initial endowments. One type of agent, called laborers, has initial endowments only of labor, with each agent having one unit. The other type of agent, called capitalists, has initial endowments only of capital, with each agent also having one unit. In addition, the ratio of capital to labor of the whole community is unity.

Assumption II: Utility functions. The utility functions of laborers and of capitalists differ. Laborers have initial endowments of labor but wish to consume capital.

The utility function of a laborer of tastes ϵ is accordingly

$$(4) \quad U = a_L + b_L K + c_L \epsilon R - d^R d^C \overline{C},$$

where $a_L \epsilon (-\infty, \infty)$, $b_L \epsilon (0, \infty)$, $c_L \epsilon (0, \infty)$, and where

d^R is a dummy variable equal to zero if the agent obeys the code of behavior of the community and equal to unity if the agent fails to obey it;

d^C is a dummy variable equal to unity if the agent believes in the code of behavior of the community and equal to zero if the agent does not believe;

K is the agent's final allocation of capital;

R is the agent's reputation; and

$\overline{C}$ is a parameter representing the loss of utility from disobeying the code of honor by a believer in the code.

According to (4), an individual who disobeys the code ($d^R = 1$) and who believes in the social values of the code ($d^C = 1$) loses utility in amount $\overline{C}$, which is a parameter. A person who disobeys the code ($d^R = 1$) but who does not believe in it ($d^C = 0$) does not lose utility directly by disobeying it, since $d^C d^R \overline{C} = 0$; however, he may lose utility from loss of reputation (as reflected in the third term in the right-hand side of (4), whose behavior will be described in further detail below). A person who obeys the code does not lose utility (i.e., the third and fourth terms on the right-hand side of (4) are both zero).

Similarly and symmetrically, capitalists have initial endowments of capital but wish to consume labor. The utility function of a capitalist is

$$(5) \quad U = a_K + b_K L + c_K R,$$

where $a_K \epsilon(-\infty, \infty)$, $b_K \epsilon(0, \infty)$, $c_K \epsilon(0, \infty)$, and where L is the agent's final allocation of labor and R is his reputation. Implicit in (5), all capitalists have the same utility function.[7]

Assumption III: Distribution of tastes. The utility function of a laborer of type ϵ is given in (4), but the distribution of tastes, i.e., of ϵ, must also be specified. ϵ is assumed to be uniformly distributed between the two positive parameter values ϵ_0 and ϵ_1.

---

7 In a more realistic model, of course, the utility functions of capitalists and laborers would be represented in a different fashion and "trade" between them would be accomplished through intermediate firms. The laborers would own labor but wish to consume goods. The capitalists would own capital but also wish to consume goods. The firms would use both capital and labor to produce goods. Considerable simplification of the model, without qualitative change of results, is achieved by eliminating goods from the utility functions and representing trade of capital for labor as occurring directly.

Assumption IV: Code of behavior. The code of behavior of the community specifies that trade of capital for labor should occur at an exchange rate $\bar{\omega}$, with $\bar{\omega} > 1$. With capital as the numeraire good, Assumption IV says that labor should be traded at the "fair wage" of $\bar{\omega}$. This particularization of the code of behavior is the simplest example that will yield unemployment. Pursuant to the "realistic story" told at the end of the introduction regarding the unwillingness of workers to cooperate in training incoming workers who undercut existing wages, there are many similar but more complicated specifications of the code that will also yield unemployment.

Assumption V: Reputation function particularized. A person loses reputation by disobeying the code of behavior of the community among those persons who believe in that code. Accordingly, let

(6) $R = 0$ if the agent obeys the code,
          $R = -\mu\bar{R}$ if the agent disobeys the code,

where

R is the agent's reputation;
μ is, as before, the fraction of the community who believe in the community's code of honor; and
$\bar{R}$ is a positive constant.

Equation (6) can be rewritten more succinctly as

(7) $R = -d^R \mu \bar{R}$,

where d^R is the dummy variable earlier defined.[8]

8 This assumption parallels the assumption in epidemiology that the number of persons who catch a disease is proportional to the number of persons who are infectious (and also to the number of persons who are susceptible). See Bailey [1957] and Bartlett [1960]. Schelling [1978] in his fascinating new book discusses at great length the structure and consequences of models in which externalities depend on the number of persons with a certain endogenously determined quality. Chapter 3 of that book discusses models of "critical mass," of which the model here is one example. The relation of loss of reputation to the number of persons who believe in the code of behavior is similar to the dependence of persons' decisions regarding neighborhood on the fraction of persons of their own race in the neighborhood (as in Schelling's "tipping" model). (See Schelling [1971, 1978].) The dual equilibria of our model are also a characteristic shared by Schelling's "tipping" model.

Assumption VI: Utility formation function particularized. Let $g(\mu, x)$ have the special form $g(\mu, x) = \beta(x - \mu)$ so that

$$(8) \quad \dot{\mu} = \beta(x - \mu),$$

where β is a positive constant. According to (8), if more persons obey the code x than believe it, the number of believers will rise. Conversely, if fewer persons obey the code than believe it, the number of believers will fall.

B. Assumptions concerning the operations of markets including definition of equilibrium

Assumption VII: Nature of markets. Markets are such that any agent may conclude any contract with any other agent. A contract is a trade of one good for another at a specified rate of exchange: in the case of this model, trade of K for L or L for K at a fixed rate of exchange (denoted ω).

Assumption VIII: Rationing mechanism. The nature of the model, which has been constructed to demonstrate involuntary unemployment, requires ipso facto the existence of some rationing. It is therefore necessary to specify how this rationing will take place. It is assumed that in an equilibrium any agent who is willing to trade at the equilibrium rationed price has an equal chance of being successful in such a trade. This is precisely the assumption made by Grossman [1971] in his theory of equilibrium of rationed markets. In Grossman's terminology, the probability that a rationed agent on the demand side of a rationed market is successful in concluding a contract is the ratio of effective supply to notional demand. Symmetrically, the probability that a rationed supplier is able to conclude a contract in a rationed market is the ratio of effective demand to notional supply.

Assumption IX: Definition of equilibrium. Equilibrium occurs, according to our definition, if there is no agent who makes a contract with another agent who could withdraw from that contract and, without making a contract with another agent, have higher utility. In addition, no two agents could withdraw from contracts with third parties and exchange among themselves, making both of them better off. Although no proof is provided, this concept of equilibrium corresponds to Grossman's concept [1971] that in markets in which goods (or factor services) are traded, effective demand must equal effective supply.

IV. Short-run equilibrium

This section discusses the determination of short-run equilibrium. By short run it is meant that μ, the fraction of persons who believe in the community's code of behavior, is fixed.

Both labor and capital can be divided into three parts: what is traded at the "fair wage" $\bar{\omega}$, denoted L_1 and K_1, respectively; what is traded at a rate ω not equal to $\bar{\omega}$, denoted L_2 and K_2, respectively; and what is not traded at all, denoted L_3 and K_3, respectively. The market for L_1 and for K_1 only clears as a matter of sheer coincidence. The supply of labor at $\bar{\omega}$ almost always exceeds the demand for labor at $\bar{\omega}$ (equal to the supply of K_1 divided by $\bar{\omega}$) or vice-versa, so that rationing must occur in either supply or demand. For a nonrationed agent, effective demand will be notional demand for all three types of capital or labor, respectively, 1, 2, and 3. On the other hand, for a rationed agent effective demand must take into account the constraint imposed by rationing. Equilibrium in this economy occurs when the effective supply of labor equals the effective demand for labor traded at $\omega \neq \bar{\omega}$. These effective demands and supplies for L_2 and K_2 take into consideration the rationing constraints on labor traded at $\bar{\omega}$; so it follows by definition that the effective demand and supply of labor and capital traded at $\bar{\omega}$ are also equal.

The first step in the argument involves the determination of the agents who are rationed. Notional demand and supply of labor can be calculated as a function of ω. The notional demand for labor is derived from budget-constrained maximization of the utility function of capitalists. Inspection of the utility function for capitalists reveals the solution to this maximizing decision. There is a threshold wage ω_{crit}. If ω is greater than this threshold, the capitalist will prefer to trade his unit of capital at $\bar{\omega}$. If ω is below this threshold, the capitalist will prefer to break the social code and trade at ω ($\neq \bar{\omega}$). This threshold is calculated by comparing the utility from trading at $\bar{\omega}$, which is $a_K + b_K/\bar{\omega}$, to the utility from trading at ω, which is $a_K + b_K/\omega - c_K\mu\bar{R}$. If the two utilities are exactly equal, each capitalist is exactly indifferent between trade at ω and trade at $\bar{\omega}$. Such equality occurs at the threshold level of ω, $\omega = \omega_{crit}$, where

$$(9) \quad \omega_{crit} = \overline{\omega}/(1 + (c_K/b_K)\mu\overline{R}\overline{\omega}).$$

Summing over all capitalists yields the notional demands for labor traded at $\overline{\omega}$ and ω:

$$(10) \quad L_1^{ND} = 0 \qquad \omega < \omega_{crit}$$
$$(11) \quad \overline{\omega}L_1^{ND} + \omega L_2^{ND} = K \qquad \omega = \omega_{crit}, \; L_1^{ND} \geq 0, \; L_2^{ND} \geq 0$$
$$(12) \quad L_1^{ND} = K/\overline{\omega} \qquad \omega > \omega_{crit}$$
$$(13) \quad L_2^{ND} = K/\omega \qquad \omega < \omega_{crit}$$
$$(14) \quad L_2^{ND} = 0 \qquad \omega > \omega_{crit},$$

where superscript ND denotes "notional demand."

The notional supply of labor is similarly calculated. A laborer wishes to trade his labor at $\overline{\omega}$ or at ω accordingly as $a_L + b_L\overline{\omega}$ is greater than or less than $a_L + b_L\omega - c_L\mu\epsilon\overline{R} - d^C\overline{C}$. According to this inequality, a laborer with $\epsilon > (b_L(\omega - \overline{\omega}) - d^C\overline{C})/c_L\mu\overline{R}$ has notional supply of labor traded at $\overline{\omega}$ of one unit. Conversely, a laborer with $\epsilon < (b_L(\omega - \overline{\omega}) - d^C\overline{C})/c_L\mu\overline{R}$ has a notional supply of labor traded at $\omega(\neq\overline{\omega})$ of one unit. Considering the distribution of tastes F, we see that

$$(15) \quad L_1^{NS} = L\{\mu(1 - F(z_l)) + (1 - \mu)(1 - F(z_l'))\}$$
$$(16) \quad L_2^{NS} = L\{\mu F(z_l) + (1 - \mu)F(z_l')\}$$
$$(17) \quad L_3^{NS} = 0,$$

where

$$z_l = (b_L(\omega - \overline{\omega}) - \overline{C})/c_L\mu\overline{R},$$
$$z_l' = b_L(\omega - \overline{\omega})/c_L\mu\overline{R},$$

and

$$F(z) = \text{proportion of population with tastes } \epsilon \leqq z.$$

L_1^{NS} and L_1^{ND} are graphed in Figure I. Note that as long as $\omega < \overline{\omega}$, the arguments of F on the right-hand side of (15) and (16) are both negative. Since ϵ is always positive, $F(z) = 0$ for $z \leqq 0$, so that $L_1^{NS} = L$ for $\omega < \overline{\omega}$; $L_2^{NS} = 0$ for $\omega < \overline{\omega}$.

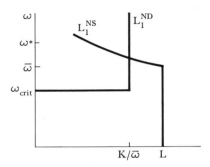

Figure I. The notional supply and demand of labor traded at $\overline{\omega}$ are plotted as a function of ω. If ω is less than ω_{crit}, all capitalists wish to buy labor at the low rate ω, therefore $L_1^{ND} = 0$. If $\omega > \omega_{crit}$, capitalists wish to trade only at $\overline{\omega}$, therefore $L_1^{ND} = K/\overline{\omega}$. If $\omega < \overline{\omega}$, all laborers would prefer to trade at $\overline{\omega}$ (rather than at ω), therefore $L_1^{NS} = L$.

Figure I therefore shows that for $\omega < \overline{\omega}$, $L_1^{NS} = L$, $L_1^{ND} \leq K/\overline{\omega}$. By Assumption I, $K/L = 1$ and by Assumption IV $\overline{\omega} > 1$, so that for $\omega < \overline{\omega}$, $L_1^{NS} > L_1^{ND}$. As a result, there is some $\omega^* > \overline{\omega}$, as pictured, such that labor demanded is greater than labor supplied for $\omega > \omega^*$; conversely, labor demanded is less than labor supplied for $\omega < \omega^*$. Below ω^*, however, the demand constraint in the trade of labor at $\overline{\omega}$ is binding. The Appendix shows that an equilibrium cannot occur with $L_2^{ED} = L_2^{ES}$ for $\omega > \omega^*$ (where superscript ED denotes *effective demand* and superscript ES denotes *effective supply*).

Since the notional demand for L_1 is less than the notional supply in the range $\omega < \omega^*$, no constraint is binding on the purchase of labor at $\overline{\omega}$, and hence the effective demand for L_1 equals the notional demand if $\omega < \omega^*$. The equations for notional demand (13), (11), and (14) become equations for effective demand, so that

(18) $L_2^{ED} = K/\omega$ $\omega < \omega_{crit}$

(19) $\overline{\omega} L_1^{ED} + \omega L_2^{ED} = K$ $\omega = \omega_{crit}$, $L_1^{ED} \geqq 0$, $L_2^{ED} \geqq 0$

(20) $L_2^{ED} = 0$ $\omega_{crit} < \omega < \omega^*$, $\omega \neq \overline{\omega}$.

The effective supply of labor traded at $\omega \neq \overline{\omega}$, L_2^{ES}, is the sum of two terms. First, if $\omega > \overline{\omega}$, there may be some persons with a notional supply of labor to be traded at ω. Second, if $\omega < \omega^*$, there will be some laborers (see Figure I) who try to trade labor at $\overline{\overline{\omega}}$ but are unsuccessful. These persons, if unsuccessful, must decide whether to trade their labor at $\omega(\neq \overline{\omega})$ and lose reputation or not to trade their labor at all.

The first term of L_2^{ES}, which is L_2^{NS} for $\omega < \omega^*$, has already been calculated and is given by (16). The second term is calculated as follows:

A laborer who offers to sell his labor at $\overline{\omega}$ has a probability of acceptance of this offer equal to L_1^{ED}/L_1^{NS} and a probability of rejection of the offer of $(1 - L_1^{ED}/L_1^{NS})$. All laborers with $\epsilon > (b_L(\omega - \overline{\omega}) - d^C \overline{C})/c_L \mu \overline{R}$ offer to trade labor at $\overline{\omega}$, as has already been seen. It remains to describe the tastes of those persons who, being unable to sell their labor at $\overline{\omega}$, instead trade at ω. The utility of a laborer who does not trade at all is a_L. The utility of a laborer who trades at $\omega \neq \overline{\omega}$ is $a_L + b_L\omega - c_L\epsilon\mu\overline{R} - d^C \overline{C}$. Accordingly, if $\epsilon < (b_L\omega - d^C \overline{C})/c_L\mu\overline{R}$, a laborer will prefer to trade at ω than not to trade at all. Consequently, all laborers with tastes ϵ between $(b_L(\omega - \overline{\omega}) - d^C \overline{C})/c_L \mu\overline{R}$ and $(b_L\omega - d^C \overline{C})/c_L\mu\overline{R}$ will have a probability $(1 - L_1^{ED}/L_1^{NS})$ of being able to trade labor at $\overline{\omega}$ and will then trade their labor at ω. As a result,

$$(21) \quad L_2^{ES}(\omega) = L(1 - L_1^{ED}/L_1^{NS})\{\mu[F(z_u) - F(z_l)] + (1 - \mu)[F(z_u') - F(z_l')]\} + L_2^{NS}(\omega),$$

where

$$z_u = (b_L\omega - \overline{C})/c_L\mu\overline{R}$$
$$z_l = (b_L(\omega - \overline{\omega}) - \overline{C})/c_L \mu\overline{R}$$
$$z_u' = b_L\omega/c_L\mu\overline{R}$$
$$z_l' = b_L(\omega - \overline{\omega})/c_L\mu\overline{R}.$$

Formula (21) specifies L_2^{ES} as a single-valued function of ω and μ for all values of $\omega \neq \omega_{crit}$, since L_1^{NS} and L_1^{ED} are single-valued functions of ω and μ for $\omega \neq \omega_{crit}$. L_2^{ED} is also a single-valued function of ω for $\omega \neq \omega_{crit}$. Any ω for which $L_2^{ES} = L_2^{ED}$ is an equilibrium. Since L_2^{ES} and L_2^{ED} are monotonic functions for $\omega \neq \omega_{crit}$, there is at most one equilibrium value of ω on either side of ω_{crit}.

For $\omega = \omega_{crit}$, L_1^{ED} is not a single-valued function. It lies anywhere between 0 and $K/\overline{\omega}$ and must satisfy $\overline{\omega}L_1^{ED} + \omega L_2^{ED} = K$. Nevertheless, there is at most one value of $L_2^{ES} = L_2^{ED}$ given $\omega = \omega_{crit}$.

This value can be calculated as follows:

$$(22) \quad L_1^{ED} = (K - \omega_{crit} L_2^{ED})/\overline{\omega}$$

whence

$$(23) \quad L_2^{ES}(\omega_{crit}) = L\{1 - (K - \omega_{crit} L_2^{ED})/\overline{\omega} L_1^{NS}\}\{\mu F(z_u) \\ + (1 - \mu)F(z_u')\},$$

where

$$z_u = (b_L \omega_{crit} - \overline{C})/c_L \mu \overline{R}$$
$$z_u' = b_L \omega_{crit}/c_L \mu \overline{R}.$$

(The terms $F(z_l)$ and $F(z_l')$ in (21) do not appear in (23), since $\omega_{crit} < \overline{\omega}$, so that z_l and z_l' are both negative; ϵ is positively distributed, so that $F(z_l) = F(z_l') = 0$.)

Using (23) and letting $L_2^{ED} = L_2^{ES}$ yields at most one equilibrium value of L_2^{ED} between 0 and K/ω_{crit}. Such a value, if it exists, is a short-run equilibrium for L_2; ω_{crit} is then a short-run equilibrium value of ω.

The formula for $L_2^{ED} = L_2^{ES}$ will be used to plot the short-run equilibrium values of L_2^{ES}/L as a function of μ. (There may be more than one such value for a given μ.) Long-run equilibrium is given where μ equals $(1 - L_2/L)$, so that the fraction of persons who obey the community's code of behavior equals the fraction of persons who believe in that code. The next section will discuss some general properties of that long-run equilibrium. Section VI will then plot L_2^{ES}/L as a function of μ, for a numerical example with given parameter values of b_K, c_K, b_L, c_L, $\overline{R}$, $\overline{C}$, ϵ_0, ϵ_1, and $\overline{\omega}$, which are the parameters of our general-equilibrium system.

V. Long-run equilibrium

In the long run the fraction of persons who obey the code $(L_1 + L_3)/L$ must equal the fraction who believe the code μ. This condition, in conjunction with the short-run condition that the effective supply of labor traded at $\omega \neq \overline{\omega}$ equal the effective demand for labor traded at $\omega \neq \overline{\omega}$, yields the long-run equilibrium conditions for the economy.

This section proves three propositions concerning this long-run equilibrium.

A. Propositions I to III briefly described

If Assumption V is modified so that the code of behavior allows persons to make any contract without loss of reputation (while all other description of the economy is unchanged), the economy will have an equilibrium at which capital is traded for labor at a rate ω equal to unity. All capital and all labor would be offered in the market, so that the effective demand for labor is K/ω, the effective supply of labor is L, and the equilibration of effective demand and supply of labor yields $K/\omega = L$, or $\omega = K/L = 1$. We view this economy, in which the code of behavior does not refer to market transactions and all other assumptions are the same, as the neoclassical economy that corresponds to our economy in all respects except the existence of the code of behavior. Proposition I states that an economy with a code of behavior (as summarized by assumptions I to IX) has at least one equilibrium which is exactly the same as that of the corresponding neoclassical economy, with $\mu = 0$ and $L_2^{ED}/L = L_2^{ES}/L = \omega = 1$ irrespective of parameter values.

Proposition II classifies long-run equilibria if reputation is unimportant; the equilibria that occur as the reputation parameter approaches zero are examined. According to Proposition II, there are two cases. In the first case, there is a unique equilibrium with $\mu = 0$ and $L_2^{ED}/L = L_2^{ES}/L = \omega = 1$. In this case the influence of reputation is necessary to maintain the social code. In the second case there are multiple equilibria in which the code is both believed and obeyed.

The parameter values that are the dividing line between the two cases yield the clue as to why they occur as they do. The first case occurs if $\overline{C} < b_L$, and the second case occurs if $\overline{C} > b_L$. If $\overline{C} > b_L$, a person who believes in the code holds a belief that is sufficiently strong for him to be willing to give up a wage of one unit in order not to betray that code. Thus, as long as the wage remains sufficiently close to one (as will occur in short-run equilibrium), any person who believes in the code will obey it, independent of any influence due to loss of reputation. Furthermore, in this case with $\overline{C} > b_L$, as long as reputation is unimportant, all persons who disbelieve the code will disobey it, and all persons who believe the code will obey it. As a result, there are multiple equilibria in which the persons who obey the code exactly coincide with the persons who believe it. In contrast, if $\overline{C} < b_L$ and the wage is sufficiently close to unity, only with sanctions imposed by loss of reputation will it pay persons who believe the code to obey it. Consequently, sanctions imposed by loss of reputation are necessary to maintain the code.

Proposition III states that as long as persons care sufficiently about reputation, so that $\overline{R}$ is sufficiently large, other parameters being given, there will be a stable equilibrium with all persons obeying the community code of behavior, with $\mu = 1$, and $L_2^{ES}/L = L_2^{ED}/L = 0$ and all trades of capital for labor occurring at $\overline{\omega}$.

B. Propositions I to III formally stated and proved

Proposition I. For $\mu = 0$, $L_2^{ES}/L = L_2^{ED}/L = 1$, $\omega = K/L = 1$ is always an equilibrium.

Proof. If $\omega = K/L = 1$ and $\mu = 0$,

$$(24) \quad \omega < \omega_{crit} = \overline{\omega}$$

by the formula for ω_{crit} (9) and Assumption IV that $\overline{\omega} > 1$.

$$(25) \quad L_2^{ED} = K/\omega, \quad \text{for } \omega < \omega_{crit}.$$

Using the formula for L_2^{ES}/L, (21), we see that the uniform distribution of ϵ between ϵ_0 and ϵ_1, and the negativity of $b_L(\omega_{crit} - \overline{\omega}) - d^C\overline{C}$ yields (26):

$$(26) \quad L_2^{ES}/L = \{(L - 0)/L\}\{\mu F(z_u) + (1 - \mu)F(z_u')\},$$

where

$$(27) \quad F(z) = 1/(\epsilon_1 - \epsilon_0)[\min(z, \epsilon_1) - \min(z, \epsilon_0)]$$

and

$$(28) \quad z_u = (b_L\omega - \overline{C})/c_L\mu\overline{R}$$
$$(29) \quad z_u' = b_L\omega/c_L\mu\overline{R}.$$

Evaluating (26) for $\mu = 0$, using (27), (28), and (29) we see that

(30) $L_2^{ES}/L = 1$.

Therefore, $L_2^{ES} = L_2^{ED} = L$, $(L_1^{ES} + L_3^{ES})/L = \mu = 0$, for $\omega = 1$, $\mu = 0$. Hence, $L_2^{ES}/L = L_2^{ED}/L = \omega = 1$, $\mu = 0$ is a long-run equilibrium.

Q.E.D.

Proposition II. If $\overline{C} < b_L$, $L_2^{ES}/L = L_2^{ED}/L = \omega = 1$ is the only short-run equilibrium as $\overline{R}$ approaches 0.

If $\overline{C} > b_L$, any μ in the range $0 \leq \mu \leq 1 - 1/\min(\overline{C}/b_L, \overline{\omega})$ is a long-run equilibrium with $\omega = 1/(1 - \mu)$ and $L_2^{ES}/L = 1 - \mu$, in the limit as $\overline{R}$ approaches 0.

Proof. The proof is divided into four parts. Parts (i) to (iii) show the uniqueness of equilibrium if $\overline{C} < b_L$. Part (i) shows that there is one and only one equilibrium for $\omega < \omega_{crit}$. Part (ii) shows that $\omega = \omega_{crit}$ cannot be an equilibrium value of ω. Part (iii) shows that $\omega > \omega_{crit}$ cannot be an equilibrium value of ω. Part (iv) shows the nature of equilibria if $\overline{C} > b_L$.

All four parts use (31) that

(31) $\lim\limits_{\overline{R} \to 0} \omega_{crit} = \overline{\omega}$,

as is apparent for the formula for ω_{crit} (9). This fact may be stored, therefore, for future reference.

Part i. There is one and only one equilibrium for $\omega < \omega_{crit}$.

If $\omega < \overline{\omega}$,

(32) $\omega < \lim\limits_{\overline{R} \to 0} \omega_{crit} = \overline{\omega}$,

hence using (21), (10), (32), and (27), we see that

(33) $L_2^{ES}/L = \mu F(z_u) + (1 - \mu)F(z_u')$,

where $F(z)$ is given by (27), z_u is given by (28) and z'_u is given by (29). Evaluating (33), we show that

(34) $\dfrac{L_2^{ES}}{L} = 1$ if $\omega > \dfrac{\overline{C}}{b_L}$

(35) $\lim\limits_{\overline{R} \to 0} \dfrac{L_2^{ES}}{L} = 1 - \mu$ if $\omega < \dfrac{\overline{C}}{b_L}$

The formula for L_2^{ED}, (18), yields

(36) $L_2^{ED}/L = K/\omega L$ for $\omega < \omega_{crit}$.

If $\omega = 1$, $\omega < \overline{\omega} = \lim_{\overline{R} \to 0} \underline{\omega}_{crit}$ (by (32) and Assumption IV that $\overline{\omega} > 1$). Hence for $\omega = 1$, if $\overline{C}/b_L < 1$,

(37) $L_2^{ES}/L = L_2^{ED}/L = K/\omega L = 1$

by (34) and (36).
  $L_2^{ES}/L = L_2^{ED}/L = \omega = 1$ is also the only short-run equilibrium for $\omega < \omega_{crit}$. If $\omega < 1$ by (34) and (35), $L_2^{ES}/L \leq 1$. By (36), $L_2^{ED}/L > 1$. Hence $L_2^{ES} \neq L_2^{ED}$, $\omega < 1$.
  Similarly, if $\omega_{crit} > \omega > 1$,

$L_2^{ES}/L = 1$ by (34) if $\overline{C}/b_L < 1$;
$L_2^{ED}/L = K/\omega L < 1$ by (36).

Hence $L_2^{ES} \neq L_2^{ED}$ for $\omega_{crit} > \omega > 1$.

Part ii. ω_{crit} is not an equilibrial value for ω for $\lim \overline{R} \to 0$.

  Suppose that $L_2^{ES} = L_2^{ED}$. We shall prove the contrary. If $\omega_{crit} < \overline{\omega}$ and if

$L_2^{ES} = L_2^{ED}$,

using (23),

(38) $L_2^{ES}/L = \{1 - (K - \omega_{crit}L_2^{ES})/\overline{\omega}L\}\{\mu F(z_u)$
$+ (1 - \mu)F(z'_u)\}$,

where $F(z)$ is given by (27) and

$$z_u = (b_L\omega_{crit} - \overline{C})/c_L\mu\overline{R}$$
$$z'_u = b_L\omega_{crit}/c_L\mu\overline{R}.$$

Letting $\overline{R} \to 0$ and evaluating L_2^{ES}/L using (38) and also (27), (28), and (29) yield

$$(39) \quad \frac{L_2^{ES}}{L} = \frac{1 - K/L\overline{\omega}}{1 - \omega_{crit}/\overline{\omega}} \, 1.$$

Since $\omega_{crit} < \overline{\omega}$ for $\overline{R} > 0$ and since $\lim_{\overline{R}\to 0} \omega_{crit} = \overline{\omega}$,

$$(40) \quad \lim_{\overline{R}\to 0} \frac{L_2^{ES}}{L} > \frac{K}{L\omega_{crit}}$$

The right-hand side of (40) is the limit of permissible values of L_2^{ED}/L by (19), so that

$$\lim_{\overline{R}\to 0} L_2^{ED} \neq L_2^{ES} \text{ for } \omega = \omega_{crit}.$$

This contradicts the assumption that $L_2^{ED} = L_2^{ES}$. Hence $\omega = \omega_{crit}$ is not an equilibrium value for ω.

Part iii. There are no equilibrium values of ω greater than ω_{crit} for $\lim \overline{R} \to 0$.

For $\omega > \omega_{crit}$,

$$(41) \quad L_2^{ES}/L = (1 - K/L\overline{\omega})\{\mu(F(z_u) - F(z_l)) + (1 - \mu)(F(z'_u) - F(z'_l))\} + \mu F(z_l) + (1 - \mu)F(z'_l),$$

where

F is given by (27)
z_u is given by (28)
z'_u is given by (29)
$z_l = (b_L(\omega - \overline{\omega}) - \overline{C})/c_L\mu\overline{R}$
$z'_l = b_L(\omega - \overline{\omega})/c_L\mu\overline{R}.$

Evaluating (41) for $\lim_{\overline{R} \to 0}$, for $\overline{C}/b_L < 1$, we see that

(42) $L_2^{ES}/L \geqq 1 - K/L\overline{\omega} > 0$ for $\omega > \omega_{crit}$;

by (20)

(43) $L_2^{ED} = 0$ for $\omega > \omega_{crit}$

so that

$$L_2^{ED} \neq L_2^{ES}   \text{for } \omega > \omega_{crit}.$$

Summarizing the conclusions of Parts (i), (ii), and (iii), for $\lim \overline{R} \to 0$, the only short-run equilibrium is $\omega = 1$, $L_2^{ED}/L = L_2^{ES}/L = 1$, with $\overline{C} < b_L$.

Part (iv). If $\overline{C} > b_L$, any μ in the range $0 \leqq \mu \leqq 1 - 1/\min (\overline{C}/b_L, \overline{\omega})$ is a long-run equilibrium with $\omega = 1/(1 - \mu)$ and $L_2^{ES}/L = 1 - \mu$ as $\overline{R} \to 0$.

By (35),

$$L_2^{ES}/L = 1 - \mu,   \text{if } \omega < \overline{C}/b_L.$$

By (36) with $\omega = 1/(1 - \mu) < \omega_{crit}$,

$$L_2^{ED}/L = (1 - \mu)K/L = 1 - \mu.$$

Hence for $0 \leqq 1/(1 - \mu) \leqq \min (\overline{C}/b_L, \overline{\omega})$, $L_2^{ES}/L = L_2^{ED}/L$— so that $\omega = 1/(1 - \mu)$ yields a short-run equilibrium as $\overline{R}$ approaches 0.

Furthermore, $L_2^{ES}/L = L_2^{ED}/L = 1 - \mu$ is a long-run equilibrium since

$$\dot{\mu} = \beta(1 - (1 - \mu) - \mu) = 0.$$

Proposition III. For $\overline{R}$ sufficiently large, other parameters being constant, there is a stable long-run equilibrium with $L_2^{ED} = L_2^{ES} = 0$ and with $\mu = 1$.

Proof. For $\overline{\omega} > \omega > \omega_{crit}$, by (21), (12), and (16),

(44) $L_2^{ES}/L = (1 - K/L\overline{\omega})\{\mu F(z_u) + (1 - \mu)F(z_u')\}$,

where $F(z)$ is given by (27), z_u is given by (28), and z_u' is given by (29). Let $\overline{R}$ be greater than $b_L\overline{\omega}/c_L\epsilon_0$. Then for $\overline{\omega} > \omega > \overline{\omega}/(1 + (c_K/b_K)\overline{R}\overline{\omega})$, by (44), with μ in a neighborhood of 1,

(45) $L_2^{ES}/L = 0$ for $\mu = 1$.

Furthermore, by (20), for $\overline{R}$ and ω so chosen

(46) $L_2^{ED} = L_2^{ES} = 0$, μ being in a neighborhood of 1.

As a result $\mu = 1$ is a long-run equilibrium with $(L_1 + L_3)/L$ also equal to one.

Furthermore, in a neighborhood of $\mu = 1$, $\mu < 1$,

(47) $\dot{\mu} = \beta((L_1 + L_3)/L - \mu) = \beta(1 - \mu) > 0$

by Assumption VI, so that $\mu = 1$ is a stable equilibrium.

Q.E.D.

VI. Graph of proportion of population obeying code as a function of proportion of believers

The propositions of the last section regarding the effect of reputation occur because the greater is the number of believers in the community's code of behavior, the greater is the incentive to obey that code. If nearly everyone believes in the code, the incentives may be sufficiently strong that nearly everyone will obey it. Whereas, if very few persons believe in the code, the incentives are apt to be sufficiently weak that virtually no one will obey it. For this reason, if reputation is sufficiently important there will always be two possible equilibria, both of which are locally stable in terms of the dynamic $\dot{\mu} = \beta((L_1 + L_3)/L - \mu)$.

Specific values of the parameters $b_L = c_L = 10$, $c_K/b_K = 0.1$, $\overline{R} = \overline{C} = 5$, $k = K/L = 1$, $\overline{\omega} = 1.25$, $\epsilon_0 = 0.5$, $\epsilon_1 = 1.5$ were chosen, and the percentage of persons obeying the code in short-run

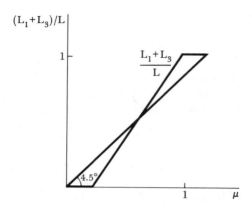

Figure II. Fraction of population that believes in the code of behavior is the 45° line. Fraction of population that obeys the code is $(L_1 + L_3)/L$. $(L_1 + L_3)/L$ is plotted as a function of μ.

equilibrium was plotted against the percentage who believed in the code, as shown in Figure II. The two stable intersections with the 45° line are at $\mu = 0$, $(L_1 + L_3)/L = 0$ and $\mu = 1$, $(L_1 + L_3)/L = 1$.

Using formula (21) for L_2^{ES} and (18), (19), and (20) for L_2^{ED}, we classified the values of ω that satisfy

$$L_2^{ES}/L = L_2^{ED}/L$$

into three types.

"Lower Roots": for which $0 < \omega < \omega_{crit}$, and

$$(48) \quad K/L\omega = \mu F(z_u) + (1 - \mu)F(z_u'),$$

where $F(z)$ is given by (27), z_u is given by (28) and z_u' is given by (29). The left-hand side of (48) represents L_2^{ED}/L for $0 < \omega < \omega_{crit}$. The right-hand-side represents L_2^{ES}/L.

"Middle Roots": for which $\omega = \omega_{crit}$, and

$$0 \leqq L_2/L \leqq K/L\omega_{crit},$$

where

$$(49) \quad \frac{L_2}{L} = \frac{(1 - K/L\overline{\omega})\{\mu F(z_u) + (1 - \mu)F(z_u')\}}{(1 - \omega_{crit}/\overline{\omega}\{\mu F)(z_u) + (1 - \mu)F(z_u')\}},$$

where

$$F(z) \text{ is given by (27)}$$
$$z_u = (b_L \omega_{crit} - \overline{C})/c_L \mu \overline{R}$$
$$z'_u = b_L \omega_{crit}/c_L \mu \overline{R}.$$

Equation (49) results from equating L_2^{ES}/L and L_2^{ED}/L and from using the relation (19), which is true for $\omega = \omega_{crit} : \overline{\omega} L_1^{ED} + \omega_{crit} L_2^{ED} = K.$

"Upper Roots": ω is an "upper root" if $\omega > \omega_{crit}$ and ω satisfies equation (50):

$$(50) \quad 0 = (1 - K/L\overline{\omega})\{\mu F(z_u) + (1 - \mu)F(z'_u)\},$$

where $F(z)$ is given by (27), z_u is given by (28) and z'_u is given by (29). The left-hand side of (50) is L_2^{ED}/L for $\omega > \omega_{crit}$. The right-hand side is L_2^{ES}/L as a function of ω for $\overline{\omega} > \omega > \omega_{crit}$.

The graph in Figure II was plotted using the solutions to these three equations ((48), (49), and (50)) in the relevant ranges of ω or L_2/L, or both.

VII. Generalization and conclusions

The model constructed here is a new class of model in which there is a code of behavior as to how persons should behave in the market and in which persons lose reputation for not behaving in accordance with such norms. This model is a compromise between those explanations of social phenomena that rest upon social custom, as much anthropological work is wont to do, and those explanations of social phenomena that rest upon economic motives, as economics, sometimes in extreme form, is wont to do. Which customs will be obeyed is partly endogenous to the model and partly due to history. A custom that is too costly to follow, in terms of lost utility, will not be followed and therefore will disappear. A custom that is fairly costless to follow will, once established, continue to be followed because persons lose utility directly by disobeying the underlying social code and also because, according to the model, disobedience of social custom results in loss of reputation.

Our paper answers the question of whether economic gains must necessarily erode social customs, the violation of which results in greater utility to persons who do not care about the obedience to the custom per se. The answer, according to our model, is that such customs may, once established, continue to be followed with a stable fraction of the population believing in those customs and also following them. In this way, we interpret the "upper" equilibrium in which a stable nonzero fraction μ believes in the society's code of behavior and also follows it.

While such has been established in the context of our model there remain many questions and much research to be done on the class of models built here. First, in the model here persons believe in the community's behavior, or they do not believe; there is no spectrum of belief. It remains an open question as to whether greater continuity in the degree of belief in social customs ipso facto results in the erosion of customs that are not economically profitable, because persons can cheat on those customs at the margin.

Second, a model of unemployment was given. This model assumed a code of behavior in which persons who failed to trade capital for labor at a fixed rate $\bar{\omega}$ were said to have violated the community's code of behavior. More realistic codes of fairness will result in more realistic models of unemployment. It remains to build and analyze such models.

Third, the existence of equilibria with stable social customs was demonstrated. It remains, however, to classify under what conditions such stable equilibria exist and also when they fail to exist. In the context of our model some attempt at such classification was made, i.e., if $\bar{R}$ is sufficiently large, such equilibria do exist; if $\bar{R}$ is sufficiently small, such equilibria exist only if persons who believe in the code have beliefs so strong that they would all lose utility by breaking it.

Fourth, utility, technology, endowments, and intergenerational utility formation were all described by very particular functions. It remains to analyze the same model with more general (or even different, although no more general) functions describing utility, technology, endowments and utility formation.

Fifth, in the model above, all persons in the community had the same code of behavior. The interaction between different, potentially conflicting subcultures is also an important aspect of the dynamics of real social systems that remains to be analyzed in a more complete model.

Finally, the community's code of behavior was taken as exogenous, and the number of believers in the code considered endogenous. A full explanation of social customs and economic equilibrium must describe not only how the system works with existing conditions, but also how such codes themselves evolve.

Appendix

There is no equilibrium for $\omega > \omega^*$.

Proof. Let ω be greater than ω^*. It will be shown that $L_2^{ES} \neq L_2^{ED}$ for $\omega > \omega^*$.

$$(51) \quad L_1^{NS} + L_2^{NS} = L$$

by (15) and (16), whence

$$(52) \quad L_2^{ES}/L = (1 - L_1^{ES}/L) \text{ for } \omega > \omega^*.$$

Using the constrained maximization of the utility function (5), we can show that

$$(53) \quad L_2^{ED}/L = (1 - L_1^{ES}/L_1^{ND})K/L\omega$$
$$\text{for } \omega^* \leq \omega \leq \max(b_K/c_K\mu\overline{R},\omega^*)$$
$$(54) \quad L_2^{ED}/L = 0 \text{ for } \omega \geq \max(b_K/c_K\mu\overline{R}, \omega^*).$$

Using (53) and (54), we see that

$$(55) \quad L_2^{ED}/L \leq (1 - L_1^{ES}/L_1^{ND})K/L\omega$$
$$(56) \quad = (1 - L_1^{ES}/K/\overline{\omega})K/L\omega, \text{ since } L_1^{ND} = K/\overline{\omega}, \omega > \omega_{crit}$$
$$(57) \quad = (1/\omega - L_1^{ES}/L\overline{\omega}/\omega) \text{ since } K/L = 1$$
$$(58) \quad \leq 1/\omega(1 - L_1^{ES}/L),$$
$$\text{since } \overline{\omega} < 1 \text{ (with strict inequality if } L_1^{ES} \neq 0),$$
$$(59) \quad \leq 1 - L_1^{ES}/L \text{ since } \omega > \omega^* > \overline{\omega}$$
$$> 1 \text{ (with strict inequality if } L_1^{ES} = 0).$$

Using (58), (59), and (52), we see that

$$L_2^{ED}/L < (1 - L_1^{ES}/L) = L_2^{ES}/L.$$

Hence $L_2^{ED} \neq L_2^{ES}$ for $\omega > \omega^*$.

Q.E.D.

London School of Economics

References

Akerlof, G. A., "The Economics of Caste and of the Rat Race and Other Woeful Tales," *Quarterly Journal of Economics,* XC (Nov. 1976), 599–618.

and D. Soskice, "The Economics of Sanctions," mimeo, Berkeley, California, December, 1976.

Arrow, K. J., "Models of Job Discrimination," in A. H. Pascal, ed., *Racial Discrimination in Economic Life* (Lexington, MA: D. C. Heath, 1972), 83–102.

Azariadis, C., "Implicit Contracts and Underemployment Equilibria," *Journal of Political Economy,* LXXXIII (Nov./Dec. 1975), 1183–1202.

Bailey, F. G., *Gifts and Poison* (New York: Shocken, 1971).

Bailey, N. T. J., *The Mathematical Theory of Epidemics* (London: Hafner Publishing, Griffith, 1957).

Baily, M. N., "Wages and Unemployment under Uncertain Demand," *Review of Economic Studies,* XLI (Jan. 1974), 37–50.

Bartlett, M. S., *Stochastic Population Models in Ecology and Epidemiology* (London: Methuen, 1960).

Becker, G. S., *The Economics of Discrimination* (Chicago: University of Chicago Press, 1957).

"A Theory of the Allocation of Time," *Economic Journal,* LXXV (Sept. 1965), 493–517.

"Crime and Punishment: An Economic Approach," *Journal of Political Economy,* LXXVI (March/April 1968), 169–217.

"A Theory of Marriage: Part I," *Journal of Political Economy,* LXXXI (July/Aug. 1973), 813–46.

"A Theory of Marriage: Part II," *Journal of Political Economy,* LXXXII (March/April, 1974), 11–26.

Benedict, R., *Patterns of Culture* (Boston: Houghton-Mifflin [Sentry Books], 1961).

Grossman, H. L., "Money, Interest and Prices in Market Disequilibrium," *Journal of Political Economy,* LXXIX (Sept./Oct. 1971), 943–61.

Hall, R. E., "The Rigidity of Wages and the Persistence of Unemployment," *Brookings Papers on Economic Activity* (1975: 2), 301–49.

Kroeber, A. L., *Anthropology* (New York: Harcourt-Brace, 1923).

Phelps, E. S., *Inflation Policy and Unemployment Theory: The Cost-Benefit Approach to Monetary Planning* (London: Macmillan, 1972).

   and S. G. Winter, eds., *Microfoundations of Employment and Inflation* (New York: Norton, 1970).

Schelling, T. C., "Dynamic Models of Segregation," *Journal of Mathematical Sociology*, I (July 1971), 143–86.

   Micromotives and Macrobehavior (New York: Norton, 1978).

Tobin, J., "Inflation and Unemployment," *American Economic Review*, LXII (March 1972), 1–18.

Veblen, T., *The Theory of the Leisure Class, An Economic Theory of the Evolution of Institutions* (New York: Macmillan, 1899).

6
Jobs as dam sites

1. Introduction

Much economic analysis is based on stylized relations between the nature of economic processes and the functions economists use as their tools of analysis. For example, if production processes are duplicable, constant returns to scale production functions are obtained. The student of elementary economics is told that if goods are difficult to substitute, their demand is inelastic; if easy to substitute their demand is elastic. In similar fashion it is the purpose of this paper to categorize the nature of jobs and to show that it has implications for the elasticity of demand for labour with respect to the wage.

We see a job as like a dam site. A dam which underutilizes a dam site, even though productive in the sense that water is usefully stored or electricity is usefully produced, will nevertheless be costly in the sense that the valuable dam site is wasted. Even at zero cost (and hence a benefit/cost ratio of infinity) it may not pay to use a dam which underutilizes the site. We picture jobs and workers in the same way. Jobs are pictured as being like dam sites and workers of different skills as being like the potential dams on the dam site. Workers of sufficiently low skills will not be able to get jobs even at zero wages, not because their output on those jobs is negative, but because they underutilize the jobs themselves. Nor may it matter that the firm will have to pay significantly positive wages to hire skilled workers on its jobs.

This image of the job gives reason for pessimism about the wage

The author would like to thank Sanford Grossman, Oliver Hart, Mervyn A. King, Hajime Miyazaki, Janet L. Yellen, and a referee for *The Review of Economic Studies* for valuable comments, and the U.S. Department of Labor for financial assistance under Small Grant No. 91-06-78-27 and the National Science Foundation under Research Grant SOC 75-23076, administered by the Institute of Business and Economic Research of the University of California, Berkeley. A previous incarnation of this paper bore the title, "A Theory of Involuntary Unemployment."

elasticity of demand for labour of a given skill, since it says that unskilled workers, no matter how low they bid their wages, may still be unable to bid jobs away from skilled workers.

This has at least five consequences. First, it shows that in a demand downturn, in which prices of final goods and services are below the full employment level, wage flexibility alone will not be sufficient to restore full employment. Skilled workers will receive jobs and positive wages; unskilled workers will not be able to capture jobs even at zero wages.

Second, the minimum wage is often considered a major cause of unemployment in general and among youth in particular (see Feldstein (1973) for one example). The effect of minimum wages on employment depends critically on the wage elasticity of demand, which is low for unskilled workers if, as in our argument, they cannot capture jobs even at zero wages.

Third, Feldstein (1973, pp. 19–26) among others has argued that wage subsidies should be paid to encourage employers to hire youths in ladder jobs. Feldstein's recommendation rests implicitly on the belief that the elasticity of demand for such youths in such jobs is fairly high – at least in the sense that employers would more than willingly hire such workers with sufficient reduction of the minimum wage. Wage costs thus serve as an upper bound to his estimates of the costs of such programmes. If, on the other hand, jobs are, as pictured in this paper, like dam sites, even at a zero wage firms may be quite unwilling to hire unskilled workers in ladder jobs because they may underutilize the ladder jobs themselves.

The other side to the subsidy issue is manpower training programmes. Such programmes have been strongly criticized in the U.S. for their high cost per worker. Implicit in much of this criticism has been the comparison with on-the-job training on the supposition that the cost of such training must necessarily be less than the wages paid in such jobs. This implicit comparison, however, is invalid according to this paper since the cost of using an unskilled worker in a job is not just the cost of his wages but the cost of his underutilization of the scarce resource, the job itself.

Fourth, the job-as-dam-site view of the labour market explains another well-known phenomenon. The unemployment rates of unskilled labour are always greater than the unemployment rates of skilled labour. There are two common explanations of this phenomenon, to which the dam site model adds a third.[1] One explanation is that money wages for jobs are rigid. When a job is vacant the employer selects from all applicants the most skilled person willing to accept the job at the rigid money wage fixed for the given job. Because of this system of selection less skilled workers do not have the option of underbidding more skilled applicants. The second explanation is Becker's (1964). Workers with greater skills, says Becker, have higher ratios of specific human capital, relative to their wage. As a consequence, in a cyclical downturn, it is suboptimal for a firm to lay off its high-specific-capital workers and potentially lose its investment if they cannot be subsequently rehired. In contrast, in the theory of this paper, skilled workers can always bid the wage for a job below the point where the unskilled worker is willing to compete – unless the unskilled worker is willing to take a negative wage, as sometimes occurs in apprenticeships.

Fifth, economists have long puzzled about the high elasticity of short-run output with respect to employment, as reflected crudely in Okun's Law, and less crudely in terms of short-run production functions. It is surprising that the short-run elasticity of output, even with respect to production workers, exceeds unity. The model of this paper gives an explanation why this phenomenon might occur. As the firm goes into the downturn of the business cycle, it may not pay to lay off all workers who produce less output than their wage, because of the loss of specific human capital and, also potentially, because of the effect on the morale of the rest of the work force. On the other hand, the marginal cost of operating the job, even at a zero wage, may exceed the value of the added output, so some workers may be effectively idled in the downturn.

This paper is organized in the following way. Section 2 is an analysis of the key features which result in nonutilization of a resource at zero cost, even though that resource is positively productive. The analogy with low grade land in the Ricardian model is exact as is the analogy with dam sites.

The third section discusses the nature of jobs. In that section the distinction (new I believe in this paper) between specific technology

1 A less-known explanation is that of Melvin Reder (1964), who explains this phenomenon as due, at least in part, to promotion ladders. Reder also gives tables that show the comparative unemployment rates by skill level.

and specific human capital is made. It is asserted, with at least some empirical backing, that the nature of job organization is a form of specific technology and, furthermore, that the usual form of such organization causes jobs to have the features which cause low-grade complementary factors (e.g. low-grade land in the Ricardian model and unskilled labour in our model) to be unutilized even at zero cost when demand is low.

Sections 4 and 5 then are specific examples of jobs as dam sites. They illustrate the low wage elasticity of the demand for unskilled labour. These two sections show that labour, which working with capital has positive marginal product, nevertheless cannot command positive wages when demand is low – because jobs are better utilized by more skilled workers, even though they earn positive wages.

2. Common features in models of nonutilization and analogy between jobs and dam sites

This paper is about conditions under which it is unprofitable to hire labour even at zero wages. These conditions occur, it is argued, if labour underutilizes jobs which themselves are valuable resources because of their potential for productivity. There are at least three examples in the economics literature where factors of production are unutilized if the complementary factors are sufficiently scarce: in the putty-clay models, in Ricardian land theory, and in cost-benefit analysis (on the utilization of given projects on fixed dam sites). The discussion of these three examples in this section will reveal their common features, which are responsible for the respective factor of production to be unutilized and command a zero return if its complementary factor is sufficiently scarce. Once the common element in these models has been exposed, the analogy between jobs and dam sites appears natural, and hence the argument that unskilled labour even at zero wages may not be profitably employed. In this way a picture of production emerges in which the wage elasticity of demand for labour is quite low.

The first example is the putty-clay model. Although the emphasis of the putty-clay literature has been on the long-run similarity of the putty-clay and the putty-putty models (Akerlof (1967), Bliss (1968), Johansen (1959), Solow (1962, 1963)), the emphasis in this literature could have been quite different. It could have concerned results that are quite special in a more general theory of production, as will be explained presently at some length.

According to this model, λ units of machines of capital-intensity λ use one unit of labour. Insofar as one unit of labour is used with that capital, another unit of labour cannot be so used. According to Solow, there is a distribution of machines of type λ, which produce an output $g(\lambda)$ when using one unit of labour. The perfectly competitive economy will allocate labour over machines in such a way that output is maximized. Thus, the perfectly competitive economy chooses the rate of utilization of machines of type λ, $\mu(\lambda)$ to maximize total output, subject to the constraint that the labour utilized cannot exceed the labour supply.

Letting Λ denote the space of all possible types of machines, and letting $f(\lambda)$ denote the distribution of machines of type λ in the economy, the perfectly competitive economy chooses $\mu(\lambda)$ to maximize

$$(1) \qquad \int_{\lambda \in \Lambda} \mu(\lambda) g(\lambda) f(\lambda) \, d\lambda,$$

subject to the constraint

$$(2) \qquad \int_{\lambda \in \Lambda} \mu(\lambda) f(\lambda) \, d\lambda \leqq L,$$

where L is the total quantity of labour in the economy.

The net result of the maximization of (1), subject to the constraint (2), is an aggregate production function that is dependent on the distribution of machines $\{f(\lambda)\}$ and the total supply of labour L. This aggregate production function will have one important qualitative property. Even though labour will have a positive product on low-capital intensive machines, as long as there is a sufficiently large number of highly capital-intensive machines, the addition of low capital-intensive machines will have no effect on aggregate output. The marginal product of such machines (in the production of aggregate output) will be zero. The reason for such zero-marginal products is easy to explain. If machines require labour to be operated, and a labourer who operates a machine must be taken from elsewhere in the economy, a sufficiently labour-intensive machine will, if used, have a negative marginal product, since the opportunity cost of the complementary inputs is greater than the value of its output.

This feature of the putty-clay model is not unique to it, and there are at least two other well-known economic models in which the same principle applies. It is worth discussing (at least briefly) these two other situations, since they will clarify the nature of the job, as described in this paper, and will explain by analogy the results obtained in this paper.

For the first analogy, consider the Ricardian model of land utilization. According to Ricardo, there is land of different grades. Land of grade λ in amount T_λ can be used to produce an output of $Q_\lambda = F_\lambda(T_\lambda, L_\lambda)$ when working with an amount of labour L_λ. Under competitive conditions, there is an aggregate output produced, Q, where:

$$(3) \quad Q = \sum_\lambda Q_\lambda = \max \sum_\lambda F_\lambda(T_\lambda, L_\lambda),$$

for given amounts T_λ of each grade of land $\lambda \epsilon \Lambda$ and with L_λ chosen to maximize (3), subject to the constraint (4):

$$(4) \quad \sum_\lambda L_\lambda \leqq L.$$

The solution to the maximization of aggregate production (3), subject to the labour constraint (4), shows that, for grades of land λ, such that

$$(5) \quad \partial F/\partial L_\lambda(T_\lambda, 0) < w,$$
$$(6) \quad L_\lambda = 0,$$

where w is the marginal product of labour in the production of aggregate output (i.e., $\partial Q/\partial L$).

In Ricardo's terms, that land which is incapable of producing an output per unit of labour equal to the wage earned elsewhere remains untilled, or in the language of the putty-clay models, is "scrapped." One condition which determines whether such scrappage occurs is whether the elasticities of substitution of land for labour in the production functions F_λ are less than unity. If these elasticities of substitution for each λ are uniformly less than one, sufficient abundance of higher-grade land leads to the scrappage of less good land (Matthews (1964)).

Note that, in general, there is an aggregate production function:

(7) $\quad Q = F(L, T_1, \ldots, T_\Lambda)$,

but this production function has a special property. According to this special property, if the quantity of land of higher grade is sufficiently abundant, land of lower grade will contribute nothing to aggregate output. This scrappage of lower-grade land occurs even though labour and lower-grade land, considered alone, both have positive marginal products. The use of the lower-grade land, however, will require the use of labour, which, in the presence of abundant high-grade land and limited substitutability, has an opportunity cost in excess of its output on the low-grade land. One reason why this result occurs is that labour, insofar as it works with one grade of land, cannot also work with another. In the same way, in the putty-clay model, if labour worked with one type of capital, it was precluded from working with another type of capital.

A job is similar. By nature, insofar as a job is filled by one person, it cannot be filled by another. In the Ricardian model, land of sufficiently poor quality that it could not produce the opportunity cost of the labour tilling it, is untilled. Correspondingly, in the model below, with jobs and with labour of different qualities, labour of such poor quality that it cannot earn the opportunity cost of the jobs it might fill will be unemployed.

A third phenomenon, which is exactly analogous to the scrappage of submarginal land in the Ricardian model, and the idling of low capital-intensive machines in the Johansen–Solow model occurs in cost-benefit analysis. The archetypal cost-benefit problem concerns whether or not to build a dam at a particular dam site. According to the usual cost-benefit analysis, the project selector should choose the project that maximizes the present discounted value of the returns of building the dam net of the costs. Projects that fail to meet this criterion, *even though they have benefit-cost ratios in excess of unity,* should not be built – for a reason that is simple to explain. Only one dam can be built on the dam site. Insofar as one dam is built, another dam can not be. For this reason, the dam site is a scarce resource. Thus, those dam proposals whose discounted returns are less than the maximum waste the dam site, even if they have benefit-cost ratios in excess of unity (with the costs calculated exclusive of the imputed rent for the dam site).

The key feature of economic structure in the dam-site example is that the dam site will take only one dam (in the Ricardian example, labour could work with only one grade of land). Insofar as it uses one dam, it cannot use another. As a result, some dams with positive net benefits (exclusive of the imputed rent on the dam site) should not be constructed. According to the title of this paper, jobs are like dam sites, insofar as a job filled by one labourer cannot be filled by another. Consequently, labourers with positive marginal products considered alone may still not be able to earn positive wages (rents), provided they make sufficiently poor use of the job (dam site). In this sense there is a low wage elasticity of demand for such labour.

3. Specific technology and jobs

The distinction between specific human capital and general human capital is well known (Becker (1964)). Human capital specific to a firm consists of knowledge that raises an individual's productivity to that firm; analogously, human capital specific to an industry raises the individual's productivity in that industry. In contrast, general human capital increases an individual's productivity wherever he works.

Analogous to the distinction between specific and general human capital is the distinction between specific and general technology. Firm-specific technology is technology specific to a particular firm; general technology is technology freely available to all firms. The difference between technology and human capital should be explained because the two concepts, which both refer to the use of knowledge, are in many respects similar.

Suppose that a firm is using a labourer with a given amount of specific human capital. If that labourer withdraws his services and is replaced by another labourer with the same general skills, the output of the firm will decline by the rent on the "lost" human capital. In contrast, suppose that a firm uses a worker with a given specific technology. If that worker leaves the firm but is replaced by a worker with the same general human capital, the output of the firm will remain the same.

A technology specifies the relation between inputs and outputs. Because returns to labour constitute approximately 75% of all value added, the relation between labour input and material output is of particular importance. One important form of specific technology is the means whereby particular firms relate labour inputs to material outputs.

It is worthwhile to make a list of types of specific technology independent of its use in this paper, because this is an important concept in its own right and worthy of exploration. But making this list also reveals an important feature of specific technology – that much specific technology consists of fixed job descriptions that relate how discrete persons (as opposed to abstract labour units, as in most economic models) relate to each other to accomplish the economic goals of the firm.

The most obvious form of specific technology is specific knowledge of production processes. In its most concrete form, such knowledge is embodied in patents issued. One indication of the order of magnitude of the input into acquiring such specific technology is given by expenditures for research and development by private industry, which, in 1976, in the United States, was $17.4 billion (U.S. Statistical Abstracts, 1979, p. 441). This compares to gross private domestic investment of $243 billion and a gross national product of $1.7 trillion. The very fact that expenditures of this magnitude were incurred by private industry at its own expense is ipso facto evidence for the existence of specific technology in nonnegligible amount.

Knowledge of production processes can be considered as a specific technology type of "hardware." In contrast, the other types of specific technology consist of systems of management and are a type of "software." There is at least one indication that this type of specific technology is an important determinant of productivity. Pratten (1976) has estimated the relative productivity levels of multinational firms with manufacturing plants in both the U.S. and Great Britain. On a firm-by-firm basis, it was found that productivity per employee was about 50% higher in the U.S. than in the U.K. In contrast, however, for all U.S. manufacturing productivity per employee, measured on a roughly comparable basis, was 116% more than in the U.K. The relatively higher productivity of the multinationals in the U.K. than that of the rest of domestic manufacturing is no doubt partly explained by the use of more inputs per person: more human capital and more capital. But the large difference in the two differentials, 116% compared to 50%, also strongly suggests that there is a large residual, which is explained by the multinationals' use in the U.K. of their specific technology.

Software-specific technology can be classified into three types. The first of these is job descriptions. All firms, either formally or informally, have sets of job descriptions that relate how one person in one job interacts with all persons in all other jobs, and also with the material inputs and outputs.

A second form of software-specific technology lies in the knowledge by the personnel of the firm as to how the firm operates. It is commonly believed that such knowledge constitutes either specific human capital, on the one hand – since the worker who leaves the firm takes that knowledge with him – or general technology, in the sense that such knowledge is common. However, it is quite common that specific aspects of a firm's operations are understood by many workers and that such knowledge is also the costless by-product of the normal pursuit of many jobs. If that is the case, it can be said that the firm owns specific technology rather than that the worker owns specific human capital. Such knowledge concerns itself with the firm's internal operations (the interrelations between the firm's work force and special knowledge about the firm's materials and capital stock) and also the firm's external operations (the markets for its goods and its inputs, including governmental interference in those markets).

A third form of software-specific technology lies in the social customs of a firm's employees. Stephen Marglin has related to me a pure example of this phenomenon. He reported visiting two cotton textile mills, one in Northern Yugoslavia, the other in Southern Yugoslavia. The capital equipment in the two factories was exactly the same. Nevertheless, in Northern Yugoslavia, each worker tended four times as many machines as did the workers in Southern Yugoslavia. If Marglin's explanation of this differential is correct, then an interchange of two workers between the north and the south would also result in an interchange of their respective productivities. Leibenstein (1976) would say that the differences in productivities were due to differences in X-efficiency.

One view of the job, as is natural in the "putty-clay" model, is that a job can be characterized by the use of a fixed number of machines. While I agree that the putty-clay model constitutes one view of the job, it is, I believe, a view more applicable to the textile industry of the nineteenth century, in which each millhand tended a fixed number of machines, than to most modern industry. In my view, most jobs consist of software, which describe the relations of one person in the firm to other persons inside and outside the firm. The key assumption in this paper is that one job could be filled by only one person (rather than, say, two or three or more). There is a reason for this, in that the interrelations of persons in different jobs (which is part of the firm's specific technology) are costly to change except in fairly rare instances or over the longer run. We believe that it is costly for firms to change job descriptions to take advantage of relative scarcities of labour and, in most cases, more costly than the advantages to be gained from reacting to flexible wages. There is some empirical support for this point of view. A study of this precise issue by Michael Piore (1968) showed that engineers in U.S. manufacturing do not consciously adjust job descriptions to take advantage of different states of the labour market. The adjustment of job descriptions in U.S. manufacturing, it must be concluded from Piore's study, occurs as a long-run rather than a short-run phenomenon.

4. A partial equilibrium example

This section illustrates, by an example, the proposition that poor labour cannot outbid good labour for a job, and thus poor labour is always unemployed prior to good labour, if there are flexible wages.

Let a job use one unit of labour of type α, with m_α units of raw materials, to produce q_α units of output. Let p_m be the price of raw materials and p_f the price of final output. Let w_α denote the wage of labour of type α. The profits of the firm in filling this job with labour of type α will be:

$$(8) \quad p_f q_\alpha - p_m m_\alpha - w_\alpha.$$

Similarly, if the firm fills the job with labour of type β, its profits will be:

$$(9) \quad p_f q_\beta - p_m m_\beta - w_\beta.$$

It is now possible to see whether a labourer of type β can underbid a labourer of type α to get the job.

As long as

$$(10) \quad p_f q_\alpha - p_m m_\alpha - w_\alpha > p_f q_\beta - p_m m_\beta - w_\beta,$$

a labourer of type α will be given the job in preference to a labourer of type β; or, alternatively, as long as

$$(11) \quad w_\beta/p_f > -q_\alpha + q_\beta + (p_m/p_f)(m_\alpha - m_\beta) + w_\alpha/p_f,$$

the job will go to labour of type α.

Alternatively stated, if the reservation wage of labour of type β is above the value of the R.H.S. of inequality (11), the type β labourer will not get the job. If a type α labourer is unambiguously more skilled than type β, he or she will both produce more output and use fewer raw materials in the job. In that case, type β's reservation wage would have to be negative if β were to capture the job if w_α/p_f is sufficiently low. In this sense, flexible wages will not guarantee jobs to unskilled labour, even if skilled labour is employed at nonzero wages.

5. A general equilibrium example

A. Remarks

The preceding example was only partial equilibrium. It showed that if a type α worker was unambiguously more productive than a type β worker, and if the wages of type α workers were sufficiently low, type β workers would not be employed, unless willing to accept negative wages. The question, however, remained as to why the wages of skilled workers might be so low. The example in this section will show that if demand (in a suitably defined sense) is low, the wages of skilled workers will also be low. Unskilled workers will be unemployed no matter how flexible their wages.

Because the purpose of the example is illustrative, there is no reason for the model to have generality. On the contrary, specificity aids in ease of computation of the equilibrium and in understanding the behaviour of the model.

B. The model

Labour. Let there be two classes of workers: skilled workers and unskilled workers. Let N_{sk} denote the total number of skilled workers and N_{un} denote the total number of unskilled workers. Skilled workers are assumed (for simplicity of the example) to be homogeneous. In contrast, unskilled workers have a distribution of abilities. These abilities, denoted by the index α, are uniformly distributed between a lowest ability of $\alpha = 0$ and a greatest ability of $\alpha = 1$. To model unemployment with perfectly flexible wages, it is assumed that all labourers have a perfectly inelastic supply of labour at any nonnegative wage.

Production. There are two types of jobs. First, there are primary jobs, which, by assumption, can be filled only by skilled workers. By assumption, these primary jobs are not homogeneous – there is a distribution of such jobs. A primary job, filled by a single skilled worker, uses one unit of raw materials and produces q units of output. The outputs have a uniform distribution between an upper bound $\bar{q}$ and a lower bound $\underline{q}$. The total number of jobs in the primary sector is J^{pr}.

In addition to primary jobs, there are secondary jobs. These jobs are all homogeneous and are J^{sec} in number. A skilled worker in one of these jobs produces an output q_{sk}^{sec}. An unskilled worker of grade α (which is uniformly distributed between 0 and 1) produces an output αq_{un}^{sec}. Consistent with the notion that skilled are more productive than unskilled, $q_{sk}^{sec} > q_{un}^{sec}$. No raw materials are used in the production of output in the secondary sector.

Markets. Output is sold in a competitive market at a price p_f and raw materials are purchased at a price p_m. It is convenient to consider these prices as internationally determined, or, alternatively, as determined by a government commodity board which buys all output at p_f and provides raw materials at price p_m. It is also convenient to consider a change in demand, as represented by a change in p_f relative to p_m, with p_f rising relative to p_m as demand rises. It will be demonstrated that as p_f rises relative to p_m, unemployment falls.

C. Comments on the model

The model has many singular features. The reason for most of these singular features is economy of modeling. Two of these singularities, as shall be discussed, are not due to a desire for simplicity of example but, instead, are intrinsic features of the model. These singular features will each be reviewed in turn.

The first singularity concerns the homogeneity of all skilled workers. This assumption is useful, since it avoids a complication. If both jobs and workers are nonhomogeneous, it is necessary to work out how nonhomogeneous workers are allocated across nonhomogeneous jobs. Although this may be a problem of some interest in general, the points of this paper can be most easily illustrated independent of the solution to that problem, by making either jobs or labour homogeneous. We have chosen, with respect to skilled workers, to make the jobs nonhomogeneous and the workers homogeneous.

The second assumption is the reverse situation in the secondary sector. All jobs in the secondary sector are homogeneous; unskilled workers, however, are nonhomogeneous. Again, the restriction of one category or the other, workers or jobs, to be homogeneous simplifies the programming problem of allocating workers across jobs. With unskilled workers being of continuous grades, it is possible to show how the unemployment rate varies continuously as the marginal worker becomes unemployed with marginal declines in demand.

Third, jobs have fixed coefficients between inputs and outputs. This assumption could be relaxed – at least somewhat. The qualitative behaviour of the model will be unchanged if there is limited substitutability between final output and material input with elasticity of substitution less than unity. In that case, the model will be more difficult to analyze, but in the limit it will behave exactly like the fixed-coefficient model. (See Akerlof (1969) for further comment on this.)

Another singular assumption concerns the use of no raw materials in secondary jobs. Indeed, the unemployment elasticities are increased if raw materials are used in secondary jobs, but skilled workers make better use of those raw materials than unskilled workers. The assumption of *no* raw materials in secondary jobs is useful to illustrate the major point of this paper in a pure way. Even though an unskilled worker has unambiguously positive output net of raw materials used in production in a secondary-sector job, such workers will nevertheless be unemployed if the demand for final output is sufficiently low, because skilled workers become less expensive to use relative to unskilled workers.

There are, however, two fixed-coefficient assumptions that cannot be relaxed if the model is to yield unemployment with perfectly flexible wages. The first of these assumptions is the availability of only a limited number of jobs: J^{pr} in the primary sector and J^{sec} in the secondary sector. The idea of the model is that as demand contracts, the number of jobs that can be profitably performed in the primary sector contracts. Skilled workers, who, in good times, would work in the primary sector, crowd into the secondary sector and compete with unskilled workers. When the total of skilled workers seeking jobs in the secondary sector and unskilled workers exceeds the number of jobs in that sector, unemployment will begin among unskilled workers. As demand contracts further, unemployment of these workers will become continually worse. If unskilled workers could produce output without a job, or if the number of jobs in the secondary sector exceeds the total of all workers (skilled and unskilled), unemployment will never develop.

The second intrinsic singular assumption in the example is the fixity of jobs and workers. If a job is performed by one worker, it cannot be performed by more than one. Insofar as one worker fills a job, another worker can only work elsewhere. This assumption is also intrinsic to the paper: it is because of this property that jobs are viewed as dam sites.

D. The analysis of the model

Because the model is kinky, its analysis must be divided into separate parts reflecting the six types of possible equilibria that can occur. With given values of other parameters, the equilibria of the economy can be plotted as a function of the state of aggregate demand as parameterized by p_f/p_m. The parameter space p_f/p_m can be divided into six separate regions (of which one or more may be empty) corresponding to the type of equilibrium. These regions, which will be described presently, are denoted Regions I to VI.

Region I. In Region I, all skilled labour is employed in the primary sector. This type of equilibrium occurs if the net revenue from the marginal job in the primary sector, with all skilled labour working in that sector, exceeds the marginal revenue from employing the first skilled labourer in the secondary sector. This type of equilibrium will occur if the number of jobs in the primary sector exceeds the number of skilled labourers and if the price of final output is sufficiently high relative to the price of raw materials.

Region II. As the price of final output, relative to raw materials, falls, it becomes relatively less profitable to hire skilled labour in the primary sector, relative to the secondary sector. With a fall in p_f/p_m, a point is eventually reached that is the boundary between Regions I and II, where the revenue on the marginal job in the primary sector, net of material costs, equals the marginal revenue product of skilled labour in the secondary sector. For ratios of p_f/p_m less than this boundary,[2] some skilled labour is used in the secondary sector. If the number of unskilled workers is less than the number of secondary-sector jobs, the influx of skilled workers into the secondary sector will not – at least in the beginning – cause any loss of employment, since there are enough jobs to go around. However, as p_f/p_m falls further, there will eventually be a point at which jobs must be rationed between the skilled workers seeking jobs in the secondary sector and the unskilled workers, provided $N_{sk} + N_{un} > J^{sec}$. The level of p_f/p_m at which such rationing begins constitutes the boundary between Region II and Region III.

Region III. In Region III, more workers are seeking jobs in the secondary sector than are available. The jobs go to the most skilled workers, with the least skilled workers unemployed. The marginal product of an employed worker is his output in a secondary-sector job, less the output of the most skilled worker who is unemployed, who would be willing to take his job (given perfectly flexible wages) at a zero wage. As p_f/p_m falls further, production in the primary sector becomes still more uneconomic, and more skilled labourers crowd into the secondary sector. Unskilled labourers become increasingly unemployed. Provided $N_{sk} > J^{sec}$, a point is eventually reached at which all unskilled labourers become unemployed. This point serves as the boundary between Regions III and IV.

Region IV. In Region IV, the use of primary-sector jobs is so uneconomic – because the price of final output has fallen so low, relative to the price of raw materials – that the number of skilled workers seeking employment in the secondary sector exceeds the number of jobs in that sector. All unskilled workers are unemployed. However, the real wage has not yet fallen to zero, but lies between $(q_{sk}^{sec} - q_{un}^{sec})$ and 0, and it equates the total demand for skilled labour in the

2 This boundary may be $+\infty$ if $N_{sk} > J^{pr}$.

primary sector and secondary sector to the total supply. Eventually, however, if p_f/p_m falls far enough, the total demand for skilled labour will be less than the total supply, even at a zero wage. The level of p_f/p_m at which this first occurs is the boundary between Regions IV and V.

Region V. In Region V, p_f/p_m is so low that, even at a zero wage, the demand for skilled workers in the primary sector is so low that more skilled workers are released from the primary sector than the total number of jobs in the secondary sector. However, some primary jobs can profitably employ workers at a zero wage.

Region VI. In Region VI, p_f/p_m is so low that no workers at all can be profitably used in the primary sector, even at a zero wage.

E. A numerical example

Rather than analyze an algebraic example with general parameter values for J^{pr}, J^{sec}, N_{sk}, N_{un}, $\bar{q}$, $\underline{q}$, q_{sk}^{sec}, and q_{un}^{sec}, we shall, in this section, analyze a particular example with numerical values for the eight parameters. For most randomly chosen examples, one or more of Region I to VI will be empty. The example chosen, however, has all six regions. It therefore captures the richness of our simple model. The parameters chosen are:

Number of jobs			Number of labourers	
Primary sector	J^{pr}	$= 10$	Skilled	$N_{sk} = 8$
Secondary sector	J^{sec}	$= 6$	Unskilled	$N_{un} = 4$
Output on most productive job in primary sector $= \bar{q} = 15$				
Output on least productive job in primary sector $= \underline{q} = 10$				
Output of skilled labour in secondary sector $= q_{sk}^{sec} = 8$				
Output of highest grade unskilled labour $= q_{un}^{sec} = 5$				

Region I. If all skilled labour is used in the primary sector, output on the marginal job is 11. The net revenue product of this marginal job is therefore:

(12) $11p_f - p_m.$

In contrast, the revenue product of the first skilled worker in a secondary job is $8p_f$. As long as

(13) $11p_f - p_m > 8p_f$,

all skilled labour is used in skilled jobs; it will receive a wage equal to $11p_f - p_m$. Unskilled labour will be hired in secondary jobs; since unskilled labour exceeds the number of those jobs (6 compared to 4), such labour will receive a real wage equal to their total output in such jobs, and no unemployment will occur.

Region II.   If

(14) $11p_f - p_m < 8p_f$,

the marginal product of the marginal skilled worker is greater in the secondary sector than in the primary sector and, therefore, some marginal skilled workers work in the secondary sector. This point is reached when

(15) $p_f/p_m = \frac{1}{3}$

No unemployment occurs, however, until more than two skilled workers seek employment in the secondary sector. This point will occur when

(16) $12p_f - p_m = 8p_f$,

or

(17) $p_f/p_m = \frac{1}{4}$

Hence, for $\frac{1}{4} < p_f/p_m < \frac{1}{3}$, the wage rate for skilled labour is $8p_f$; the wage rate of unskilled labour of grade α, $0 \leqq \alpha \leqq 1$, is $5\alpha p_f$. All labour is employed.

Region III.   For $p_f/p_m < \frac{1}{4}$ there is some unemployment. The wage of a skilled worker is his output, less the output of the marginal worker α_{min} who would alternatively take his place in a secondary sector job. Thus, if $\alpha_{min} < 1$, his wage is

(18) $\quad w_{sk} = 8p_f - 5\alpha_{min}p_f.$

Simultaneously, we can compute α_{min}. With a wage of skilled labour of w_{sk}, the marginal job in the primary sector has an output of q_{min}, where

(19) $\quad p_f q_{min} = w_{sk} + p_m.$

Employment in the primary sector (given the density of jobs in that sector) and given (18) and (19), will be

(20) $\quad E_{sk}^{pr} = 2(15 - q_{min})$
(21) $\qquad\quad = 2(15 - (w_{sk} + p_m)/p_f)$
(22) $\qquad\quad = 2(15 - 8 + 5\alpha_{min} - p_m/p_f).$

Thus, the number of skilled workers seeking jobs in the secondary sector is

(23) $\quad N_{sk} - E_{sk}^{pr} = 8 - 2(15 - 8 + 5\alpha_{min} - p_m/p_f).$

But, knowing the number of skilled workers in the secondary sector, it is possible to compute the number of secondary jobs left over for unskilled workers, which will be

(24) $\quad J^{sec} - \{N_{sk} - E_{sk}^{pr}\}$
$\qquad\qquad = 6 - [8 - 2\{15 - 8 + 5\alpha_{min} - p_m/p_f\}].$

The number of jobs filled by unskilled workers is, according to the definition of α_{min},

(25) $\quad (1 - \alpha_{min})N_{un} = (1 - \alpha_{min})4.$

Hence,

(26) $\quad (1 - \alpha_{min})4 = 6 - [8 - 2\{15 - 8 + 5\alpha_{min} - p_m/p_f\}].$

Solving for α_{min} yields

(27) $\alpha_{min} = \frac{1}{2}(p_m/p_f - 4)$.

Equation (27) yields the unemployment rate for unskilled workers for p_f/p_m in the range where $0 \leqq \alpha_{min} \leqq 1$, or in the range

$\frac{1}{11} \leqq p_f/p_m \leqq \frac{1}{4}$.

Region IV.   In this region, $\frac{1}{13} \leqq p_f/p_m \leqq \frac{1}{11}$, the wage earned by skilled workers is such as to equate the supply equal to the demand. At a wage, $0 \leqq w_{sk} \leqq 3p_f$, the demand for skilled workers in the primary sector is

(28) $2(15 - (w_{sk} + p_m)/p_f)$,

and the demand for skilled workers in the secondary sector corresponds to the number of jobs, which is 4. Consequently, the wage w_{sk} which equates the demand of skilled workers to the supply is given by:

(29) $2(15 - w_{sk}/p_f - p_m/p_f) + 4 = 8$,

so that the equilibrium wage is

(30) $w_{sk}/p_f = 13 - p_m/p_f$.

For $p_f/p_m < \frac{1}{13}$, the supply of skilled labour exceeds the number of jobs at a zero wage and, consequently, $p_f/p_m = \frac{1}{13}$ is the boundary point between Regions IV and V.

Region V. $\frac{1}{15} \leqq p_m/p_f \leqq \frac{1}{13}$. It is easily checked that, for p_m/p_f in this region, the demand for labour at a zero wage is less than the supply. At a zero wage, some primary jobs have a positive revenue product, as do all secondary jobs. However, for $p_f/p_m = \frac{1}{15}$, even the most productive job in the primary sector has zero marginal product. For this reason, $p_f/p_m = \frac{1}{15}$ is the boundary between Regions V and VI.

Region VI.   In Region VI, $p_f/p_m < \frac{1}{15}$. All skilled labour works in the secondary sector and wages are zero.

6. Summary and conclusion

According to this paper, firms own jobs. The key property of a job is that it can be filled by only one worker, just as a dam site can be filled by only one dam in our analogy. If the price of skilled workers is low enough, unskilled workers, no matter how flexible their wages, cannot bid away jobs from the skilled workers. An example was given, in which declines in demand caused the real wages of skilled workers to decline and, as a result of the competition from skilled workers, unskilled workers became unemployed. This image of production, in which job descriptions only change slowly is naturally associated with a low wage elasticity of demand for unskilled workers. The introduction listed some of the many important consequences of pessimism regarding the size of this elasticity.

References

Akerlof, G. A. (1967), "Stability, Marginal Products, Putty, and Clay," in Shell, K. (ed.) *Essays on the Theory of Optimal Economic Growth* (Cambridge, Mass.; London: MIT Press), 281–294.

Akerlof, G. A. (1969), "Structural Unemployment in a Neoclassical Framework," *Journal of Political Economy, 77*, 399–407.

Becker, G. S. (1964) *Human Capital: A Theoretical and Empirical Analysis, with Special Reference to Education* (New York: Columbia University Press).

Bliss, C. J. (1968), "On Putty-Clay," *Review of Economic Studies, 35*, 105–132.

Feldstein, M. S. (1973) *Lowering the Permanent Rate of Unemployment,* U.S. Congress, Joint Economic Committee (Washington: Government Printing Office).

Johansen, L. (1959), "Substitution Versus Fixed Production Coefficients in the Theory of Economic Growth: A Synthesis," *Econometrica 27*, 157–176.

Leibenstein, H. (1976) *Beyond Economic Man: A New Foundation for Microeconomics* (Cambridge, Mass: Harvard University Press).

Matthews, R. C. O. (1964), "The New View of Investment: Comment," *Quarterly Journal of Economics, 78*, 164–172.

Piore, M. J. (1968), "The Impact of the Labor Market upon the Design and Selection of Productivity Techniques within the Manufacturing Plant," *Quarterly Journal of Economics, 82*, 602–620.

Pratten, C. F. (1976) *Labor Productivity Differentials within International Companies* (Cambridge: Cambridge University Press).

Reder, M. W. (1964), "Wage Structure and Structural Unemployment," *Review of Economic Studies*, **31**, 309–322.

Solow, R. M. (1962), "Substitution and Fixed Proportions in the Theory of Capital," *Review of Economic Studies*, **29**, 207–218.

Solow, R. M. (1963), "Heterogeneous Capital and Smooth Production Functions: An Experimental Study," *Econometrica*, **31**, 623–645.

U.S. Department of Commerce, Bureau of the Census. (1979) *Statistical Abstracts of the United States*, Vol. 99 (Washington: Government Printing Office). 1978.

7

The economic consequences of cognitive dissonance

GEORGE A. AKERLOF AND WILLIAM T. DICKENS

Since the publication of *The Wealth of Nations,* economists have built an entire profession on a single powerful theory of human behavior based on a few simple assumptions. That model has been fruitfully applied to a wide range of problems.

But, while economists have been elaborating their analysis, keeping their basic behavioral assumptions the same, sociologists, anthropologists, political scientists, and psychologists have been developing and validating models based on very different assumptions.

For most types of economic behavior, the economists' model is probably quite adequate.[1] The models developed by other social scientists are generally ill-suited for direct incorporation into economic analysis. Nevertheless, insofar as studies in these other disciplines establish that people do not behave as economists assume they do, economics should endeavor to incorporate these observations.

This paper presents an example of how this might be accomplished in one special case. Psychologists have devoted considerable attention to the theory of cognitive dissonance. This theory has been used earlier by Albert Hirschman (1965) to describe attitude changes toward modernization in the course of development. Our paper expands the economic applications of cognitive dissonance and analyzes its welfare consequences in a formal model.

University of California-Berkeley. We would like to thank Allen Berger, Robert Clower, Jack Hirshleifer, Bernard Saffran, and Janet Yellen for valuable comments.

1 The approach of this paper to what economists might call the economics of "irrational" behavior differs from that of Gary Becker (1962). Becker views irrational behavior as random deviations from economic rationality. We use the findings of the psychologists who view irrational behavior as predictable, and therefore not totally random. Welfare implications seem to follow from the predictability of such behavior.

I. An overview

A. The basic premises

To begin, we must translate the psychological theory into concepts amenable to incorporation into an economic model. We think the theory of cognitive dissonance can be fairly represented in economists' terms in three propositions: First, persons not only have preferences over states of the world, but also over their beliefs about the state of the world. Second, persons have some control over their beliefs; not only are people able to exercise some choice about beliefs given available information, they can also manipulate their own beliefs by selecting sources of information likely to confirm "desired" beliefs. Third, it is of practical importance for the application of our theory that beliefs once chosen persist over time.[2]

In the next section we will give a brief summary of results from studies in social psychology which show that people in certain circumstances behave according to each of these three premises.

B. The fundamental model

The meaning of each of these premises and a practical application are illustrated by a model given in Section III. A great deal of anecdotal information suggests that workers in dangerous jobs are often quite oblivious to the dangers that are involved.[3] In this regard, interviews with benzene workers, some of whom denied that they were working with dangerous chemical substances, are typical (see Daniel Ben-Horin, 1979). Alternatively, Brian Main has related to us his experience in a nuclear plant where workers were given specially designed safety badges to collect information on radiation exposure in a weekly checkup. All workers in this plant, some of whom were Ph.D.s, failed to wear these badges; they were put in workers' desks

---

2 Actually, these assumptions allow for a much richer type of behavior than simple cognitive dissonance. Some of the "applications" in Section IV take advantage of this.

3 Another possible explanation for this phenomenon is that workers have noisy estimates of the safety of different jobs. In this case, there will be a tendency for workers who take a job to be those who underestimate its danger. Some of the implications of such a model have been considered in Dickens (1981).

and only brought out for the weekly checkup. Howard Kunreuther et al. (1978) related similar tales regarding failure of persons with high risk of flood or earthquake damage to purchase flood or earthquake insurance.

The model presented in Section III is constructed as an explanation for such phenomena. In that model, people prefer to believe that their work is safe. This corresponds to the first premise that workers have preferences over their states of beliefs. Workers make a choice about whether to believe the activity is safe or not safe. This accords with the second premise that workers have a choice about their beliefs. There is a benefit to believing that a job is safe, but also a cost. Those who choose to believe the job is safe do not experience the unpleasant feelings of constant fear or unsettling doubts about how wise it was to take such a dangerous job. On the other hand, if they convince themselves the job is safe, they may make costly judgment errors due to the discrepancy between their beliefs and the true state of the world.

In our model the cost of believing that work is safe is the possibility of making a mistake in the choice of safety practice. The worker chooses his beliefs according to whether the benefit exceeds the cost, or vice versa. If the psychological benefit of suppressing one's fear in a particular activity exceeds the cost due to increased chances of accident, the worker will believe the activity to be safe. Otherwise he will believe it to be unsafe. (This model assumes that the worker's beliefs are totally plastic: he can believe whatever he chooses irrespective of the information available to him. Of course this is a polar case. More complicated and general models would endow persons with a set of beliefs that may be chosen given the available information. Given his total choice set the agent chooses beliefs, and other things, to maximize his utility.)

A model of such a decision process is presented in Section III. It is analyzed with respect to how wages and labor supply will respond to the introduction of new safety equipment. The effects of safety legislation are also considered, as are the conditions under which such legislation will cause a Pareto-superior shift in the use of resources.

This paper is not to be interpreted as suggesting that cognitive dissonance is a significant feature of every economic transaction. On the contrary, in the model presented in Section II cognitive dissonance reactions are self-limiting. In most economic transactions there is no gain to rationalizing and cognitive dissonance plays no role. There are, however, special circumstances in which the assumptions mentioned in Section II will apply and cognitive dissonance will play an important role.

Besides safety regulation, we believe cognitive dissonance may be important in understanding innovation, advertising, crime, and Social Security legislation. These applications are potentially of great importance; they are, however, much more speculative than the straightforward application of our model to safety legislation. Section IV explains these applications. Section V then gives conclusions.

II. Psychological evidence for the basic premises

Much social psychology is based on the theory of cognitive consistency. At the most abstract level this means that persons are uncomfortable in maintaining two seemingly contradictory ideas. Cognitive dissonance theory is one application of cognitive consistency theory. In practice most cognitive dissonance reactions stem from peoples' view of themselves as "smart, nice people." Information that conflicts with this image tends to be ignored, rejected, or accommodated by changes in other beliefs.[4] Among other applications, persons who have made decisions tend to discard information that would suggest such decisions are in error because the cognition that the decision might be in error is in conflict with the cognition that ego is a smart person. Cognitive dissonance theory would suggest that persons in dangerous jobs must decide between two conflicting cognitions. According to one cognition, ego is a smart person who would not choose to work in an unsafe place. If the worker continues to work in the dangerous job, he will try to reject the cognition that the job is dangerous.

The question naturally arises whether the behavior that psychologists label as cognitive dissonance could be considered instead as rational behavior under Bayesian decision theory. Agents with cognitive dissonance reactions have posterior distributions that are unwarranted solely by the information available to them. Their estimate of the state of the world is influenced by their preferences over their state of belief. Using Bayesian decision rules, agents' estimates

---

4 The description of cognitive dissonance in this paper as well as our choice of which experiments to present owes a great deal to the excellent book by Elliott Aronson (1979).

of the state of the world is only influenced by the information available to them and their preferences over states of the world, but these estimates are independent of their preferences for beliefs per se. The typical psychological experiment motivated by cognitive dissonance theory compares the beliefs of two groups of agents – one a control group and the other a group whose preferences for different beliefs have been changed by the experimenter. The experimenter attempts to change these preferences while no new information is imparted to this second group that could be considered relevant to their estimate of the state of the world. From our examination of the evidence, we find it all but impossible to give a Bayesian interpretation to the results of many of the experiments, because it is all but impossible to give an explanation of the relevance of the differences in information available to the two groups.

This paper relies heavily on our three premises, for which there is supporting data from psychological experiments. The presentation of just a bit of this data is useful not only because it lends support to the three premises but also because it shows the types of situations in which cognitive dissonance reactions will be likely to occur. It should be understood, however, that the following paragraphs are merely illustrative. In their brevity, they fail to give the best possible evidence for our three premises and for the theory: That evidence being the great number of experimental results which are easily explained in terms of cognitive dissonance.

Experiments show that groups of persons with the same information have systematically different beliefs that accord with natural theories about their preferences. For example, persons like to view themselves as having made correct decisions. Interviews of bettors at a race track (Robert Knox and James Inkster, 1968) indicate that persons just leaving the betting window place much higher odds on "their horse" than persons in the queue just prior to their bet. As another example, in an experiment, an investigator (Jack Brehm, 1956) asked women to rate the worthiness of two appliances. They were then allowed to choose between the two appliances, which were given *wrapped* to the women. A few minutes later with the appliances still wrapped the women were asked for a second evaluation. These evaluations systematically changed in favor of the appliance that had been chosen.

Many laboratory examples concern immoral or cruel behavior. One experiment (Keith Davis and Edward Jones, 1960) asked students to watch another student being interviewed and then tell this student he was shallow, untrustworthy, and dull. The students who engaged in such behavior systematically changed their attitudes against the object of their cruelty. In terms of our first two premises, persons prefer to think of themselves as nice people. This self-image can be preserved if they have a low opinion of the object of their cruelty. They revise their opinions accordingly. A similar experiment (David Glass, 1964) reports that students who gave electrical shocks to victims lowered their opinion of their victims.

The cognitive dissonance model not only predicts systematic differences in interpretation of given information but also systematic differences in receptivity to new information according to preferences. In one example (Jerald Jellison and Judson Mills, 1967), some women were first asked to rate a group of products. They were then asked to choose between two of these products of quite different desirability. Before this choice was final, however, one group of these subjects was presented with information on the rejected product and a second group was presented with information on a product that had been similarly rated but had not been one of the possible choices. Curiously, the subjects for whom the information was irrelevant to their decision spent more time reading it than the subjects for whom the information was relevant. This is one of many experiments that purport to show a biased receptivity to new information.

We should not lose sight of our third premise: that the effects of cognitive dissonance on beliefs may be long lasting. It is claimed as one application of cognitive dissonance theory that persons who justify to themselves some difficult undertaking are likely to have a strong and persistent belief that the undertaking is a good one. If an undertaking is difficult and the external reward is small (in comparison to the effort involved), the individual must either justify the undertaking to himself or consider himself stupid to engage in it. Many experiments show such effects over a short time; one particular experiment (Danny Axsom and Joel Cooper, 1980) shows that these effects may be quite long lasting. Two groups of women engaged in two weight-reduction programs, both for four weeks, one involving much effort, the other involving little effort. Over the four weeks, both programs were equally effective in weight reduction. However, a year later the women in the high-effort program had an average weight loss of eight pounds, while those in the low-effort program had on an average lost virtually nothing. We consider this as evidence that cognitive dissonance may well have long-lasting effects.

III. A model

A. General description of the model

This section presents and analyzes a simple model to show the economic consequences of cognitive dissonance. There are two periods. In the first period, workers have a choice between working in a hazardous job or working in a safe job. The worker will choose the job with the highest combined pecuniary and nonpecuniary benefits.

In the first period, workers in the hazardous industry have no choice but to face the possibility of an accident as there is no safety equipment available. If the cost imposed by future wrong decisions is not too great, workers in the hazardous industry will, because of cognitive dissonance, come to believe that the job is really safe.

In the second period, cost-effective safety equipment becomes available. But, because by then workers in the hazardous industry believe the jobs to be safe, they will not purchase the equipment. Safety legislation is needed to restore Pareto optimality since the workers have an incorrect assessment of the marginal rate of substitution between safety equipment and money income.[5]

In this model, both labor markets and product markets are competitive. Also, workers begin with rational expectations. These workers know upon taking a job in the hazardous industry that they will experience cognitive dissonance and alter their estimated probabilities of accident. The purpose of building such a "complete information" model is not realism; we would not expect people to be aware of their future behavior.[6] Rather, the purpose of this assumption is to show that even in a model where workers entering a hazardous job perfectly foresee their future psychological reactions to the unsafe conditions, there may be a welfare-improving role for safety legislation. Such a role is obvious in models without rational expectations in which governments have more information than private agents.

The assumptions of our model are presented in Part B; the model is analyzed in Part C; in Part D the resulting equilibrium is illustrated; in Part E the nature of the equilibrium and the effects of the introduction of safety legislation are discussed. Initially, in Parts B,

---

5 We assume that workers cannot precommit themselves to buy the safety equipment. That assumption is analyzed in Section III.F.

6 The implications of models where people are not completely aware of their future behavior are considered in fn. 8.

C, D, and E, it is assumed that workers do not make contracts which precommit them to purchase safety equipment. Part F discusses that assumption and its implications.

B. Assumptions of the model

The assumptions of the model are given in four parts: the description of the demand for labor in the safe industry; the description of the demand for the product of the hazardous industry; the description of the nonpecuniary disadvantages of the hazardous jobs; and the description of the individual worker's psychological choice.

The labor market in the safe industry.   The safe industry is pictured as large relative to the hazardous industry. A job in the safe industry pays a fixed wage, denoted w_s. This wage anchors the wage of workers in the hazardous industry in both periods 1 and 2; that wage is determined by an appropriate equality between the pecuniary plus nonpecuniary benefits in safe and in hazardous jobs.

The demand for the product and the supply of the product in the hazardous industry.   The demand for the product of the hazardous industry in each period is given by a downward-sloping demand function $D = D(p_h)$, where D is the demand for the good and p_h is the price of the good. The good is produced by labor alone. One worker produces one unit of the good in each period. The producers are competitive, so that the supply of the good is infinitely elastic at the wage in each period.

The nonpecuniary disadvantages of work in the hazardous industry.   Without safety equipment, all workers in the hazardous industry have a probability q of accident in periods 1 and 2. The cost of an accident to a worker is c_a.

In the first period, no safety equipment is available. In the second period, a worker in the hazardous industry can purchase a new safety device which eliminates the possibility of an accident at a cost c_s. To make this equipment economically relevant, it is assumed that $qc_a > c_s$. We will also assume that workers cannot precommit themselves to purchase this safety equipment. They must decide at the beginning of the second period. The effect of relaxing this assumption and the reasonableness of doing so are considered in Part F. (Note also that in a competitive model it makes no difference whether workers or firms purchase the safety equipment.)

In addition, each worker in the hazardous industry in each period has a psychic cost of fear, equal to $c_f f$, where c_f is the unit cost of fear and f is the level of the worker's fear. (As an expositional convenience the uncomfortable feeling of a worker in a job believed to be unsafe is called "fear." This convention should not mask the relevance of our model for the economic consequences of cognitive dissonance. Cognitive dissonance theory has a more complex explanation than animalistic fear for the worker's uncomfortable feeling; he is torn between two cognitions: that he is a smart person and yet has chosen to work in a hazardous job. The welfare implications and market solution are independent of the precise description of the uncomfortable emotion.)

The relation between fear and perceived probability of accident q^* and the worker's choice of q^*. In general, f will be a function of q^*, the worker's subjective assessment of the probability of an accident occurring during the period. This function is assumed to be of the form

(1) $\quad f = q^*/q$

over the range $0 \leq q^* \leq q$. For each worker, prior to his choice between work in the hazardous or safe industry, q^* starts off equal to q, the true probability of an accident. But, cognitive dissonance is modeled by letting each worker choose any value of q^* in the range between 0 and q. However, once that choice has been made, the worker must behave as if the new value of q^* is the true probability of accident. In this model workers are fully aware of the decision environment: they have rational expectations.

C. Description of the equilibrium of the model

It is easy to analyze the equilibrium of the model by working backwards from period 2. Formal proof that the equilibrium accords with the description given here is available in an appendix on request from the authors. The proof is outlined here. The analysis of the equilibrium proceeds according to four propositions.

Proposition 1. *The wage in the hazardous industry in period 2 is w_s + c_s.*

Because real costs of producing in the hazardous industry in the second period are lower than in the first period due to the introduction of the new safety equipment, the price of the good will be lower in the second period, and therefore the demand will be higher. As a result, more of the good will be produced and hence more workers hired in period 2 than in period 1. Of necessity, the marginal worker in period 2 must come from the safe industry. Such a worker believes $q^* = q$ and will therefore purchase the safety equipment. This worker must be compensated for the wage lost from not taking a safe job, w_s, and also for purchasing safety equipment at cost c_s. Such compensation makes the two jobs exactly comparable. Thus the wage in the hazardous industry in period 2 is $w_s + c_s$.

Proposition 2. *A worker in the hazardous industry in period 2 chooses to buy safety equipment if*

$$(2) \quad q^* > qc_s/(qc_a + c_f).$$

The worker buys safety equipment in period 2 if the perceived cost of fear and the perceived cost of accident exceeds the cost of the safety equipment. The level of fear is q^*/q. The cost of fear is therefore $(q^*/q)c_f$. The perceived cost of accident is q^*c_a. Thus the worker chooses to purchase (or not purchase) safety equipment accordingly as $q^*c_a + (q^*/q)c_f$ is greater than (or less than) c_s. Inequality (2) follows.

Proposition 3. *A worker in the hazardous industry in period 1 chooses*

$$(3) \quad q^* = 0$$
if $(qc_a - c_s) < c_s c_f/(qc_a + c_f)$,
$$(4) \quad q^* = qc_s/(qc_a + c_f)$$
if $(qc_a - c_s) > c_s c_f/(qc_a + c_f)$.

The variable q^* is chosen by each worker in period 1 to maximize his welfare. The worker correctly perceives that if he chooses q^*

below the critical level $qc_s/(qc_a + c_f)$ he will make the wrong decision in period 2 regarding the purchase of safety equipment.

A worker who chooses q^* in the range below the critical level $qc_s/(qc_a + c_f)$ should choose $q^* = 0$, the level which minimizes his fear. The cost to him of fear in this case is 0, but the cost of making the wrong decision in period 2 regarding the purchase of safety equipment is

$$(5) \quad qc_a - c_s$$

and will be the same for any value of $q^* < qc_s/(qc_a + c_f)$.

Alternatively, the worker could maintain q^* sufficiently high so that he will correctly purchase safety equipment. This will occur as long as $q^* > qc_s/(qc_a + c_f)$ according to Proposition 2. And $q^* = qc_s/(qc_a + c_f)$ will minimize the cost of fear.

What value of q^* should the worker choose? To maximize his combined pecuniary and nonpecuniary income he should compare the cost of fear at the level $q^* = qc_s/(qc_a + c_f)$ to the cost of failure to purchase safety equipment at $q^* = 0$. The cost of fear at $q^* = qc_s/(qc_a + c_f)$ is $(q^*/q)c_f$, or

$$(6) \quad c_s c_f/(qc_a + c_f).$$

Accordingly the worker should choose $q^* = 0$ if (6) exceeds (5) and $q^* = qc_s/(qc_a + c_f)$ if (5) exceeds (6).

Proposition 4. *The wage of workers employed in the hazardous industry in period 1 is*

$$(7) \quad w_{h_1} = w_s + qc_a + min(qc_a - c_s, c_s c_f/(qc_a + c_f)).$$

In Case I where the worker chooses $q^* = 0$, he must be compensated for the expected costs due to accidents (qc_a) in period 1 and for the cost of making a wrong decision in period 2. A worker with a safe job in period 2 receives a wage w_s. A worker in the hazardous industry receives a wage $w_s + c_s$. A worker in the hazardous industry who does not purchase safety equipment in period 2 receives total net benefits $w_s + c_s - qc_a$. Thus for a worker in the hazardous industry to receive the same net benefits over the two periods as a worker in the safe industry, he must receive a wage in the first period

(8) $w_{h_1} = w_s + qc_a + (qc_a - c_s)$.

In Case II, where the worker chooses $q^* = qc_s/(qc_a + c_f)$, he buys safety equipment in period 2 at a cost c_s and he receives a wage $w_s + c_s$. Therefore his net benefits in period 2 are exactly the same as those of a worker in the safe industry. In period 1, however, he has an additional cost of accident equal to qc_a and an additional cost of fear equal to $(q^*/q)c_f$. Thus he must receive additional compensation relative to a worker in the safe industry in amount $qc_a + c_s c_f/(qc_a + c_f)$ so that

(9) $w_{h_1} = w_s + qc_a + c_s c_f/(qc_a + c_f)$.

Put together, these cases yield the proposition.

D. Illustration of the equilibrium

Figure 1 illustrates this equilibrium. In each period the demand for workers in the hazardous industry exactly equals the demand for the good, because it takes one worker to produce one unit of the good. In the first period there is an infinitely elastic supply of workers at the reservation wage

(10) $w_{h_1} = w_s + qc_a + min(qc_a - c_s, c_s c_f/(qc_a + c_f))$.

Thus the equilibrium wage in the first period is $w_s + qc_a + min(qc_a - c_s, c_s c_f/(qc_a + c_f))$. In the second period, there are two possible supply curves for labor. In Case I with $q^* = 0$ workers supply labor up to quantity $D(w_{h_1})$ at wage rate w_s; beyond $D(w_{h_1})$ there is an infinite supply of labor from the safe industry at wage $w_s + c_s$. In Case II with $q^* = qc_s/(qc_a + c_f)$, there is an infinite supply of labor to the hazardous industry at the wage $w_s + c_s$. In both Cases I and II, the equilibrium wage in the second period is $w_s + c_s$ because the demand curve for labor meets each of the two possible supply curves to the right of $D(w_{h_1})$ where labor supply is infinitely elastic at wage $w_s + c_s$.

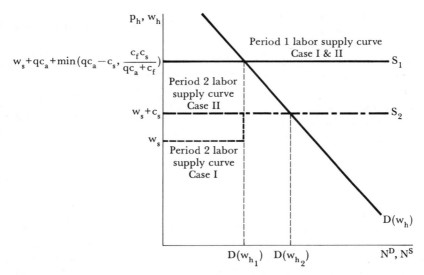

Figure 1. Labor demand and supply in the hazardous industry for periods 1 and 2.

E. The equilibrium discussed; introduction of safety legislation

What are the distributional implications of this equilibrium? First, all workers no matter what their employment history will have the same expected pecuniary and nonpecuniary income when summed over the two periods: $2w_s$.[7] When the relative costs of safety, fear, and accidents are such that all workers will choose to buy the safety equipment in the second period, all workers will have an expected income of exactly w_s in each period. If the parameters of the decision problem are such that workers in the hazardous industry in the first period will choose not to buy the safety equipment in the second period, the situation will be somewhat different. Those workers will perceive themselves as earning $w_s + c_s$ in the second period when in fact their expected income will be

$$(11) \quad w_s + c_s - qc_a < w_s.$$

7 Workers in the safe industry receive a wage of w_s in each period for a total net benefit of $2w_s$.

However, because they foresaw this eventuality at the beginning of the first period, their first-period wages compensated them for this loss. Thus the introduction of the consideration of cognitive dissonance does not change the distribution of utility among workers. What about the distribution between workers and consumers?

We now compare the equilibrium just derived to one with safety legislation. This safety legislation requires the purchase of safety equipment which has been found to be cost effective. In this case the reservation wage for working in the hazardous industry in the first period will be only

$$(12) \quad w'_{h_1} = w_s + qc_a.$$

Since workers know that they will be required to adopt the new safety technology they will always choose $q^* = 0$ and will experience no fear in the first period. Since they will be required to purchase safety equipment in the second period, they will not require compensation for making a wrong decision in period 2 or for keeping fear at a level that will allow them to buy safety equipment when available. With safety equipment, the reservation wage for all workers in the second period will be $w_{h_2} = w_s + c_s$. The wage in the second period will be the same with and without safety legislation:

$$(13) \quad w_{h_2} = w'_{h_2} = w_s + c_s.$$

The net change over the two periods due to safety legislation is a lower wage in the hazardous industry in the first period – hence a lower price of the good produced by this industry.

With safety legislation the workers still have the same expected income summed over both periods, $2w_s$. But, consumers are better off since they pay a lower price for the good of the hazardous industry in the first period. Thus safety legislation causes a Pareto-superior result.[8] If consumers have constant marginal utility of income the

---

8 Customers are the beneficiaries of safety legislation only if workers perfectly foresee their future behavior. If workers are unaware of the impending improvement in safety technology, the effect of fear, or the possibility of changing their beliefs, then the benefit of safety legislation, if any, will go to workers in the hazardous industry. That gain will be $qc_a - c_s$ per worker and will obtain in all cases where workers decide to believe that their jobs are not dangerous during the first period.

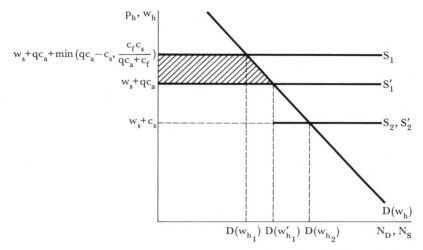

Figure 2. Labor demand and supply in the hazardous industry with and without safety legislation. The shaded area illustrates the welfare gain from legislation; the S are supply curves without safety legislation; the S' are supply curves with safety legislation.

welfare gain from safety legislation is equal to the shaded area in Figure 2.

F. Precommitment contracts

Jack Hirshleifer has pointed out to us that, in a perfect foresight world, if workers can enter into contracts at the beginning of period 1 which will bind them to purchase safety equipment in the second period, a Pareto-optimal equilibrium can be obtained through the voluntary actions of the workers without government intervention. Whether or not such precommitment contracts are possible depends on the nature of the legal system. If recontracting is allowed in the second period, workers may try to precommit themselves but will want to recontract at the beginning of the second period. Such recontracting must lead to a Pareto-optimal result given the workers' tastes

That would be all situations where the cost of fear is greater than $qc_a - c_s$, and all cases where workers do not know that they may change their beliefs or are unaware of the effect of that choice on their decision to buy safety equipment in the second period.

and beliefs *as they stand at the beginning of the second period.* Thus, if workers have taken advantage of their precommitment by allowing themselves to come to believe that their job is safe they will now want to break their contract. If recontracting is allowed, they may do so by paying some amount (less than c_s) to the person with whom they contracted. If the workers have rational expectations and a correct perception of the true model in the first period, as we have assumed, they will perceive the futility of precommitment in the presence of possibilities for recontracting and will refrain from trying.

However, in a model where agents acquire reputations from past dealings, precommitments may be viable. Agents who sell safety equipment may not be willing to recontract if by so doing they would jeopardize their reputations, thereby reducing their possibilities for advantageous future precommitment contracts. But, a model in which reputation plays a role ipso facto involves an institutional framework different from the usual competitive model and is likely to have non-Pareto-optimal outcomes.

Finally, if we relax the assumption that workers can foresee their cognitive dissonance reactions, then precommitment contracts become impossible.

IV. Potential applications

The model described in the last section is illustrative of the use of psychological findings in economic models. In this section we suggest some other applications for similar models. Some of these potential applications are directly motivated by cognitive dissonance theory. Others are merely suggested by the economic interpretation we have given that psychological theory.

A. Sources of innovation

Our model describes an economic theory of the choice of beliefs: initially, beliefs are only adopted if the net pecuniary and psychic benefits are positive. Because of cognitive dissonance, beliefs are persistent once adopted. Persons tend to avoid or resist new information that contradicts already established beliefs. As an application, this model yields some insight into the economics of innovation. In the context of the last section, in Case I, the innovators who purchased the new safety equipment in period 2 were not workers familiar by experience with the conditions of the hazardous industry, but, instead, were new workers, who in period 1 worked in the safe industry and then transferred in period 2.

The prediction from the model that innovators are previous outsiders to an activity agrees with two observations. First, in the history of science, Thomas Kuhn (1963) has claimed that the persons who first adopt a new scientific paradigm are predominantly new entrants into the field. In the field of industrial organization, it is believed that industrial laboratories are responsible for much minor innovation, but the major innovations mainly come from outside (Edwin Mansfield, 1968, p. 92). John Jewkes et al. (1959) found that prior to World War II only twelve out of the sixty-one major inventions in their study came from industrial laboratories. Over half came from private individuals. Daniel Hamberg (1963) reports similar findings after World War II.

B. Advertising

How does advertising work? Why do companies spend millions of dollars on advertising campaigns and why are people more likely to buy an advertised brand than one which does not advertise, all other things held equal?

This is undoubtedly a complicated question with answers dependent on the particular products and situations. But, the textbooks on advertising emphasize one factor: advertisements convey information about the product. The term "information," as used here, does not only refer to facts about the physical attributes of the advertised product. Advertising may also convey information about the social significance of consuming the product and how it may serve the psychological needs of consumers as well as their physical needs.[9]

If the information provided by ads generally allowed people to distinguish the functional or psychological value of a product, then it would be easy to understand how it worked to help determine peoples' choices. But, advertising textbooks admit that there are cases when the information conveyed in ads is irrelevant.

9 For example, one undergraduate text on advertising suggests that, "Consumers often expect marketing entities to perform for them, both in an overt physical sense as well as in a psychological sense. Most marketing entities promise some sort of specific psychological satisfaction as well as physical performance" (William Weilbacher, 1979, p. 159).

For example, one undergraduate advertising text divides products into three categories: those with significant differences in physical performance, those that differ only in "design or formulation characteristics" (Weilbacher, p. 174), and "generic" products or those that are "if not identical, at least indistinguishable from each other" (Weilbacher, p. 178). When brands in the latter category (and to some degree in the second category) claim a distinction from other brands, the claim is based "on the pre-emption of a quality or ingredient common to or inherent in all of the individuals in the category or on some abstract or even imagined quality" (Weilbacher, pp. 179, 181). Products that the author sees as belonging in this last category are some of the most heavily advertised. Another book suggests that there are two ways to meet consumers' desires once they have been identified. First, a new product can be created. The authors refer to this as a "product strategy." As an alternative they advise their readers that they might want to adopt an "advertising strategy" with the goal of changing "the consumers' perceptions" of an existing product so that it would be seen as filling those needs (see David Aaker and John Myers, 1975, p. 158). Finally, although the advertising texts would like to treat peoples' psychological needs as being fully commensurate with the "overt physical" needs, it is clear that at least with respect to the relevance of the information about the products conveyed by ads, they are not. The trunk size or head room of a car is relevant to someone buying a car if they carry large loads or are tall. A car with a large trunk or high ceiling may be more valuable than one without these attributes. However, the type of toothpaste that an individual uses is going to do little to affect how socially acceptable he may be. Likewise, the type of soft drink one brings usually does not affect the fun of a picnic.

If the information conveyed by ads of this type is of so little value, why would anyone ever pay attention to them?

The theory of belief proposed in this paper suggests an explanation for this phenomenon. As the advertising practitioners point out, people do have needs and tastes and they do buy goods to satisfy them. Some of these needs and tastes are quite obscure or subtle; it may be hard to tell when the needs are being met. In such cases people may *want* to believe that what they have just bought meets their needs. Advertisements give people some external justification for believing just that. People like to feel that they are attractive, socially adept, and intelligent. It makes them feel good to hold such beliefs about themselves. Ads facilitate such beliefs – if the person buys the advertised product.

This formulation also suggests a limitation to the power of advertising. People may be willing to pay a little more for a product with an attractive fantasy attached. However, there are limits to their willingness to pay. When the value of the belief is less than the additional cost of the advertised brand, advertising will fail. Such a view of advertising suggests an approach to the welfare analysis of advertising different from that in the advertising textbooks and also in the economics literature (Richard Schmalensee, 1972).

C. Social Security

Another application of this type of model of potential economic importance concerns old age insurance. Social Security legislation is based on the belief that persons left to their own devices tend to purchase too little old age insurance.

If there are some persons who would simply prefer not to contemplate a time when their earning power is diminished, and if the very fact of saving for old age forces persons into such contemplations, there is an argument for compulsory old age insurance. The case, as we see it, is analogous to the case for safety legislation made in the last section. In that model workers found it uncomfortable to contemplate the dangers involved in working in the hazardous industry. For that reason they sometimes failed to have the appropriate marginal rate of substitution between safety and wages. In a similar mode persons may find it uncomfortable to contemplate their old age. For that reason they may make the wrong tradeoff, given their own preferences, between current consumption and savings for retirement.

D. Economic theory of crime

One application of cognitive dissonance theory is to the economic theory of crime. According to Gordon Tullock (1974), the economists' theory of crime involves a straightforward application of standard price theory:

> Most economists who give serious thought to the problem of crime immediately come to the conclusion that punishment will indeed deter crime. The reason is perfectly simple. . . . If you increase the

cost of something, less will be consumed. Thus, if you increase the cost of committing a crime, there will be fewer crimes. [pp. 104–105]

Psychological experiments motivated by cognitive dissonance theory strongly suggest that Tullock's conclusions are only partially correct. While it may be true that less obedience will be observed when there is greater deterrence, these experiments show that once the threat of punishment is removed, people who have been threatened with relatively severe punishment are more likely to disobey than those threatened with relatively mild punishment.

In an experiment that has been performed under a variety of conditions, children are told not to play with a very desirable toy. One group is threatened with severe punishment; and another with mild punishment for disobedience. The children are then allowed to play in the room with the toy for some time. Later (in one experiment several weeks later; see Jonathan Freedman, 1965), the children are again put in the room with the toy, only this time without the threat of punishment. Those who have been threatened with the more severe punishment are more likely to play with the forbidden toy than those threatened with mild punishment. It has similarly been shown that children who are punished severely for aggressive behavior at home are more violent in school than those who are mildly punished (see Robert Sears et al., 1953).

The interpretation of these studies is that those who obey rules for which the penalty of violation is relatively small need to create an internal justification for their actions. When they get into a situation where external sanctions for violating the rule are reduced or eliminated, they are less likely to break the rule because they are inhibited by the internal justifications they created in the first situation.

Thus the application of price theory to crime is not so natural as Tullock, and also Becker (1968), would have us believe. Increased punishment may act as a deterrent where its effect is obvious and the probability of apprehension for crime is well understood by the criminal. But most crime is committed with the expectation by the criminal that he will not be caught. Thus self-motivation to obey the law is undoubtedly a key factor in the reduction of crime – and this may decrease with the severity of punishment.

V. Conclusion

This paper has provided an example of how psychological theory can be incorporated into theoretical economic models. In particular, a decision model motivated by cognitive dissonance theory has been constructed that is a modification of the usual model of rational decision making.

This model closely follows standard economic analysis insofar as persons are completely informed about the potential consequences of their actions and make their decisions to maximize their own welfare. But, analysis that takes account of cognitive dissonance gives different results from the standard analysis, and, in particular, provides better explanations for some phenomena that are a puzzle according to the standard approach.

For example, the approach in this paper suggests a good reason why noninformational advertising is effective, why Social Security legislation and safety legislation are popular, and also why persons fail to purchase actuarially beneficial flood and earthquake insurance. The explanations do not rely on an assumption that people are basically misinformed – if they believe something other than the truth, they do so by their own choice.

References

Aaker, David A., and Myers, John G., *Advertising Management,* Englewood Cliffs, N.J.: Prentice-Hall, 1975.

Aronson, Elliot, *The Social Animal,* 3d ed., San Francisco: W. H. Freeman, 1979.
    and Carlsmith, J. Merrill, "Effect of the Severity of Threat on the Devaluation of Forbidden Behavior," *Journal of Abnormal and Social Psychology,* June 1963, 66, 584–88.

Axsom, Danny, and Cooper, Joel, "Reducing Weight by Reducing Dissonance: The Role of Effort Justification in Inducing Weight Loss," in Elliot Aronson, ed., *Readings for the Social Animal,* 3d ed., San Francisco: W. H. Freeman, 1980.

Becker, Gary S., "Irrational Behavior and Economic Theory," *Journal of Political Economy,* February 1962, 70, 1–13.
    "Crime and Punishment: An Economic Approach," *Journal of Political Economy,* March/April 1968, 86, 169–27.

Ben-Horin, Daniel, "Dying to Work: Occupational Cynicism Plagues Chemical Workers," *In These Times*, June 27/July 3, 1979, *3*, 24.

Brehm, Jack, "Postdecision Changes in the Desirability of Alternatives," *Journal of Abnormal Social Psychology*, May 1956, *52*, 384–89.

Davis, Keith, and Jones, Edward E., "Changes in Interpersonal Perception as a Means of Reducing Cognitive Dissonance," *Journal of Abnormal and Social Psychology*, November 1960, *61*, 402–10.

Dickens, William T., "A Little Learning is a Dangerous Thing . . . ," mimeo., Berkeley, January 1981.

Freedman, Jonathan, "Long-term Behavioral Effects of Cognitive Dissonance," *Journal of Experimental Social Psychology*, April 1965, *1*, 14–55.

Glass, David, "Changes in Liking as a Means of Reducing Cognitive Discrepancies between Self-Esteem and Aggression," *Journal of Personality*, December 1964, *32*, 531–49.

Hamberg, Daniel, "Invention in the Industrial Research Laboratory," *Journal of Political Economy*, April 1963, *71*, 95–115.

Hirschman, Albert O., "Obstacles to Development: A Classification and a Quasi-Vanishing Act." *Economic Development and Cultural Change*, July 1965, *13*, 385–93.

Jellison, Jerald M., and Mills, Judson, "Effect of Similarity and Fortune of the Other on Attraction," *Journal of Personality and Social Psychology*, April 1967, *5*, 459–63.

Jewkes, John; Sawers, David; and Stillerman, Richard, *The Sources of Invention*, New York: St. Martin's Press, 1959.

Knox, Robert E., and Inkster, James A., "Postdecision Dissonance at Post Time," *Journal of Personality and Social Psychology*, April 1968, Part 1, *8*, 319–23.

Kuhn, Thomas S., *The Structure of Scientific Revolutions*, Chicago: University of Chicago Press, 1963.

Kunreuther, Howard et al., *Disaster Insurance Protection: Public Policy Lessons*, New York 1978.

Mansfield, Edwin, *The Economics of Technological Change*, New York: Norton, 1968.

Schmalensee, Richard L., *The Economics of Advertising*, Amsterdam: North Holland, 1972.

Sears, Robert et al., "Some Child-Rearing Antecedents of Aggression and Dependency in Young Children," *Genetic Psychology Monographs*, First Half, 1953, 135–234.

Tullock, Gordon, "Does Punishment Deter Crime?" *Public Interest*, Summer 1974, *36*, 103–11.

Weilbacher, William M., *Advertising*, New York: Macmillan, 1979.

8

Labor contracts as partial gift exchange

This paper explains involuntary unemployment in terms of the response of firms to workers' group behavior. Workers' effort depends upon the norms determining a fair day's work. In order to affect those norms, firms may pay more than the market-clearing wage. Industries that pay consistently more than the market-clearing wage are primary, and those that pay only the market-clearing wage are secondary. Thus, this paper also gives a theory for division of labor markets between primary and secondary.

I. Introduction

In a study of social relations among workers at a utility company in the eastern United States, George Homans [1953, 1954] observed that a small group of young women (doing a job called "cash posting") exceeded the minimum work standards of the firm by a significant margin (i.e., on average by 15 percent). Most of these women neither desired nor expected promotion in the firm in return for their troubles. Why did they do it?

Section II shows that the standard neoclassical model cannot simultaneously explain both the behavior of the firm and the behavior of the cash posters. But, as shown in Section III, application of a standard sociological model does explain the behavior of both the young women and their employer. According to this model, in their interaction workers acquire sentiment for each other and also for the firm. As a consequence of sentiment for the firm, the workers acquire utility for an exchange of "gifts" with the firm – the amount of utility depending upon the so-called "norms" of gift exchange. On the worker's side, the "gift" given is work in excess of the minimum work standard; and on the firm's side the "gift" given is wages in excess of

The author would like to thank William Dickens, Brian Main, Hajime Miyazaki, Janet L. Yellen, and two referees for invaluable help. He would also like to thank the National Science Foundation for generous financial support under Research Grant SOC 79-05562, administered by the Institute of Business and Economic Research of the University of California, Berkeley.

145

what these women could receive if they left their current jobs. As a consequence of worker sentiment for one another, the firm cannot deal with each worker individually, but rather must at least to some extent treat the group of workers with the same norms, collectively.

Norm-gift-exchange models have been used in many sociological studies to explain the behavior of workers. And these explanations are simple; properly understood, they are in tune with everyone's personal experiences of human behavior, so that they can be taken to have considerable generality. For that reason I feel confident in extrapolating such behavior beyond the narrow and particular instance of the "cash posters" to concern wage bargains and work conditions in some generality. Sections IV and V verbally explore the consequences of such behavior for wage determination; Sections VI and VII build formal mathematical models; and Section VIII gives conclusions.

This model of the microeconomics of the labor market is used to explain two phenomena that have not been successfully analyzed by more conventional economic theory. First, in most other analyses of unemployment, such as that of search theory [Phelps *et al.*, 1970], all unemployment is voluntary. In my analysis there are primary labor markets in which unemployed workers are unable to obtain jobs at the prevailing market wages. Second, the theory of dual labor markets [Doeringer and Piore, 1971] brings up the question as to which markets will be primary and which markets secondary. In the formal models developed in this paper, it is endogenously determined whether a market will be primary or secondary. Primary markets are those in which the gift component of labor input and wages is sizeable, and therefore wages are not market-clearing. Secondary labor markets are those in which wages are market-clearing.

The major feature of the usual model of implicit contracts due to Azariadis [1975] and Baily [1974] is risk-sharing agreements by the contracting agents over a span of time. These models have been taken as a vehicle for Okun's [1981, p. 133] description of labor and customer markets. This paper offers an alternative microfoundation for implicit contracts. Its emphasis is sociological. It focuses on the gift-exchange nature of employment arrangements, where the exchange is based partially on norms of behavior that are endogenously determined. This dependence of implicit contracts on *norms* of behavior (rather than on risk sharing) captures important aspects of Okun's description [1975, 1981] that have not been analyzed in the Azariadis-Baily framework.

According to this paper, norms of work effort are a major determinant of output. In emphasizing effort, it carries further the work of Leibenstein [1976] on X-efficiency. The focus on effort could also be expressed in Marxian terminology via the distinction between *labor power* and *labor* as in Edwards' recent book [1979] on the inevitable conflict between labor and management over the use of labor power.[1] In Edwards' terms this paper gives equilibrium models of the resolution of this conflict. Finally, it should be mentioned, Hirschman's concepts of *Exit, Voice,* and *Loyalty* [1970] can be expressed in terms of norms and gift exchange.

II. The nonneoclassical behavior of the cash posters or of the Eastern Utilities Co.

Economists usually assume that labor is hired as a factor of production and is put to work like capital. There is, however, one fundamental difference between labor and capital that is ignored by this assumption. Once a capitalist has hired capital, he is, over a fairly wide latitude, free to use it (or abuse it) as he wishes. However, having hired a laborer, management faces considerable restriction on how it can use its labor. Not only are there legal restrictions (such as OSHA regulations, child labor laws, etc.), but the willing cooperation of labor itself must usually be obtained for the firm to make the best use of the labor services.

Of course, standard economic theory does describe the nature of contracts when there are many possible standards of performance. According to standard theory, when a firm hires a laborer, there is an understanding by both parties that certain minimum standards of performance must be met. Furthermore, the contract may be *implicit* in the sense that workers need not be currently rewarded for their current performance but may earn chances for promotion with higher pay in the future in return for good performance in their current jobs. If this is the case, the firm need not have tight rules regarding work and compensation that very carefully specify the *quid pro quo* of pay for work, since injustices in the present can be compensated later. So standard theory can serve as a good approximation to reality even where very specific contracts relating effort or output to compensation would be quite expensive.

1 For a review of the Marxian literature on this distinction, also see Edwards [1979].

Against this background let us consider the study by Homans of "The Cash Posters." In this study a group of ten young women working as cash posters for a utility company in a New England city were interviewed and closely observed over a period of six months. The duty of a cash poster at Eastern Utilities was to record customers' payments on ledger cards at the time of receipt. The company's standard for such cash posting was 300 per hour, and careful records were made of the speed at which individual cash posters variously worked. Anyone who worked below the rate of 300 per hour received a mild rebuke from the supervisor. Table I, adapted from Homans' article, "The Cash Posters," shows both the number of cash postings per hour of different workers and their rate of error.

Note from Table I that the average number of cash postings per hour (353) was 17.7 percent greater than the standard set by the company. The simple neoclassical theory of contracts cannot simultaneously explain why the faster persons did not reduce their speed to the standard; or, alternatively, why the firm did not increase the speed expected of its faster workers. The possibility that the faster workers worked harder than the standard for either increased pay or promotion was belied by the uniformity of wage for all cash posters and by the refusal of promotion by two cash posters. When promotion did occur, it was normally to a job considered more responsible than cash posting, but nevertheless paying the same wage. In addition, voluntary quits among the cash posters were quite frequent (with most of the young women leaving to be married), so that in most cases promotion was not a relevant consideration. Since pay was not dependent on effort and promotion was rarely a consideration, the standard economic model of contract would predict that workers set their work habits to meet the company's minimum standards of performance as long as they have marginal disutility for work at that level. On the other hand, if workers do have positive utility for work at this level, the lack of incentives for effort given by the firm should lead them to choose to work to the point where the marginal disutility of additional effort is just zero. But in that case the firm could increase its profits by increasing work standards for the faster workers. Unless their utility function is discontinuous, they would still prefer their current jobs to what they could obtain elsewhere at somewhat faster speeds of work.

Since output is easily observable, it is at least a bit surprising from the point of view of the neoclassical theory of contracts that workers

Table 1. *Work performance of individual cash posters*

	Age in years	Time on job in years-months	Mean cards per hour	Mean errors per hour
Asnault	22	3–5	363	0.57
Burke	26	2–5	306	0.66
Coughlin	20	2–0	342	0.40
Donovan	20	1–9	308	0.79
Granara	21	1–3	438	0.65
Lo Presti	25	–11	317	0.03
Murphy	19	–7	439	0.62
Rourke	17	–4	323	0.82
Shaugnessy	23	–2	333	0.44
Urquhart	18	–2	361	0.49
Average	21.1	1–4	353	0.55

are not paid wages proportional to their outputs. This constitutes another puzzlement regarding the system of industrial relations among the cash posters at Eastern Utilities, although a potential answer has been suggested by Etzioni [1971]. According to Etzioni, workers find pecuniary incentives, such as piece rates, "alienating."

The mysterious behavior of the cash posters and of Eastern Utilities in terms of neoclassical theory can be posed a bit more formally. Suppose for whatever reason (perhaps Etzioni's) that the firm has decided to pay the same wage $w = \overline{w}$ to all cash posters. Further, suppose that workers have a utility function $u(w, e)$, where w is the wage rate and e is effort. Workers, mindful of the firm's work rules, should choose their effort e to maximize

(1) $u(w,e)$,

subject to the constraints,

(2) $w = \overline{w}$
(3) $e \geqq e_{min}$,

where $\overline{w} = \$1.05$ per hour, the wage fixed for all cash posters, and e_{min} is the minimum effort necessary to accomplish the required 300 cash postings per hour.

Solution of this trivial maximization problem yields

(4) $e = e_{min}$

as long as $u_e < 0$ for $e \geqq e_{min}$. On the assumption that utility is convex, there are two potential types of solutions. Each poses an empirical problem. If $u_e (\overline{w}, e_{min}) < 0$, the question arises – why did the workers not reduce their effort to 300 per hour? On the other hand, if $u_e (\overline{w}, e_{min}) > 0$, so that workers choose $u_e = 0$, why did the firm not raise the minimum standards for different workers above the point where $u_e = 0$? In either case the observation obtained is inconsistent with the neoclassical model.[2]

Of course, each cash poster may have a different utility function, and for some reason the firm may find it optimal to set the same minimum standard for all workers. For example, the rate perhaps cannot be set higher than 300 per hour in deference to the two workers who find the standard a bit onerous (as shown by Burke's and Donovan's performance in Table I, only 2 percent above the 300 minimum). But the question of why the same standard should be set for all workers can be answered only in terms of the interactions of workers among themselves and also with the firm. It is precisely in such terms that the next section poses the solution to the cash poster mystery.

Other potential objections such as the nonobservability of output and risk aversion by workers can be all but ruled out. Workers kept records of their outputs so output was easily observable, and workers did not work faster than the minimum out of fear of being sacked for falling below the minimum; as already mentioned, falling below the minimum occasioned no more than mild rebuke.

An explanation for either the firm's behavior or the workers' behavior must depend either on maximization of something other than profits by the firm or on interaction of the workers with each other and with the firm that alters their utility functions. It is to such a theory that we now turn.

---

2 The argument is just a bit subtle. If a worker with convex utility and positive marginal product for effort has a positive utility for wage income and zero disutility for added effort, the firm can increase his compensation and force him to work harder, to the advantage of both. If the worker was satisfied with his job before this additional trade, he will be even more satisfied afterwards, and therefore less willing to quit.

III. Sociological explanation of cash posters' – Eastern Utilities' behavior

The previous section showed behavior by the cash posters inconsistent with a simple neoclassical theory of worker utility maximization and firm profit maximization. I do not doubt that there is some neoclassical model involving turnover costs or difficulty of observation[3] which can explain the behavior of the firm and the cash posters, but given the failure of the simple model, the adequate model must of necessity be complicated. In contrast, this section presents a simple sociological explanation of the joint behavior of the cash posters and the Eastern Utilities Company.

According to a prominent school of sociological thought, the determinant of workers' effort is the norm of the work group. According to Elton Mayo [1949, p. 70], referring to the famous studies at the Hawthorne plant in the Bank Wiring Observation Room, "the working group as a whole actually determined the output of individual workers by reference to a standard, predetermined but clearly stated, that represented the group's conception of a fair day's work. The standard was rarely, if ever, in accord with the standards of the efficiency engineers."

According to an alternative, but equivalent, view of the cash posters' performance, they give a *gift* to the firm of work in excess of the minimum work required of 300 per hour. Offhand, it may seem absurd to view the worker as giving the firm a gift of any part of his work. Of course, the worker does not strictly give his labor as a gift to the firm; he expects a wage in return and, if not paid, will almost certainly sue in court. Likewise, the firm does not give the wage strictly as a gift. If the worker consistently fails to meet certain minimum standards, he will almost surely be dismissed. But above these minimum standards the worker's performance is freely determined. The norm (or "standard" as Mayo termed it) for the proper work effort is quite like the norm that determines the standards for gift giving at Christmas. Such gift giving is a trading relationship – in the sense that if one side of the exchange does not live up to expectations, the other side is also likely to curtail its activities.

3 For an interesting explanation of unemployment due to imperfect information, see Stoft [1980]. Solow [1980] supports the view that involuntary unemployment must be explained by sociological models of behavior.

The classic anthropological literature on the gift, particularly the essay by Marcel Mauss [1954], emphasizes this reciprocal nature of gift giving.[4] Mauss points out that, in the two major branches of Western European languages, the root for *poison* is the same as the root for *gift*, since in ancient German the word *gift* means both gift and poison, and the Greek word δόσις for poison, which is the root of the English *dose*, has the same root as the Greek word *to give*. The reason for the close association of the words for *gift* and *poison* in these ancient languages comes from the obligatory nature of reciprocity of a gift, or, equivalently, the threat of harm that was believed to befall a recipient who failed to reciprocate. Although the magic has gone out of the sanctions behind repayment of most gifts, there are probably few in modern times who have never received a gift they did not want or who have not given a gift they considered to be inadequately appreciated.[5]

Why should there be any portion of labor that is given as a gift to the firm or of treatment of the worker by the firm that can be considered a gift? The answer to this question is at once trivial and profound. Persons who work for an institution (a firm in this case) tend to develop sentiment for their co-workers and for that institution; to a great extent they anthropomorphize these institutions (e.g., "the friendly bank"). For the same reasons that persons (brothers, for example) share gifts as showing sentiment for each other, it is natural that persons have utility for making gifts to institutions for which they have sentiment. Furthermore, if workers have an interest in the welfare of their co-workers, they gain utility if the firm relaxes pressure on the workers who are hard pressed; in return for reducing such pressure, better workers are often willing to work harder.

The giving of gifts is almost always determined by norms of behavior. In most cases the gift given is approximately in the range of what

---

4 A good, although not recent, review of the anthropology and sociology of gift exchange is Belshaw [1965]. See also Titmuss [1971].

5 It has been suggested to me by one referee that the analysis of labor contracts as partial gift exchange relates to the Freeman-Medoff argument [1979] on trade unions as collective voice. Reciprocal gift giving induces union formation because discontented workers find it more difficult to quit and find another job with gift giving than without. As in Mauss's analysis it is suggested that reciprocal gift giving, i.e., mutual benevolence and dependence, go together with mutual hostility and militancy.

the recipient expects, and he reciprocates in kind. The norms of gift giving are determined by the relationship between the parties; thus, for example, it is expected that an increase in workers' productivity will be rewarded by increased wages to the workers. Much of union wage negotiations concerns the question of what constitutes a *fair* wage. To an economist who believes that wages are market-clearing or only determined by the relative bargaining power of the contractual parties, long discussions about the "fair wage" should have no bearing on the final settlement. But this notion neglects the fact that the average worker works harder than necessary according to the firm's work rules, and in return for this donation of goodwill and effort, he expects a fair wage from the firm.

This view of wages–effort as mutually reciprocal *gifts* leaves several unanswered questions. The firm decides not only work rules but also wages for each and every worker. Why should not Eastern Utilities set high standards of minimum effort and terminate all workers who are not capable of meeting or who are not willing to meet that standard (for example, Burke and Donovan in Table I)? Again there is a simple answer. In working together, workers acquire sentiment for each other. An increase in minimum standards that would put pressure on Burke and Donovan might easily be considered by the group as a whole as failure by the firm to reciprocate the group's collective donation of productivity 17.7 percent in excess of the minimum requirements. Indeed, although the details are unclear in Homans' account, there is indication that such a situation had arisen with respect to the cash posters. As Homans reports, "a couple of years before, when relations between the posters and a former division head were strained, there may have been some restriction on output."

In a different context, that of a soldier in basic training in World War II, it is revealed most clearly why better workers come to the aid of their fellows:

If one is so favored by nature or training that he gets much more done, or done better, than his neighbor, he shows up that neighbor. The neighbor then gets rebukes or extra work. One cannot do this to any decent fellow who is trying his best, especially when you have to live side by side with him and watch his difficulties and sufferings. Therefore, the superior person – if he has any heart at all and if he is sensitive to the attitudes of his barracks mates –

will help his less able neighbor to get along [Stouffer *et al.,* 1949, Vol. 2, p. 414].

Of course the cash posters were working under less extreme conditions. Nevertheless, they undoubtedly could have expressed their own reasons for helping each other in similar terms.

I have indicated the nature of the trade between firms and workers that is exemplified in the case study of the cash posters and that gives a consistent and plausible explanation for the behavior of both the firm and the workers; this explanation tells why workers exceed the minimum standards of work on the one hand, and why the firm does not raise these minimum standards on the other hand. But work standards are only one dimension of the treatment of workers. Another dimension is wages. For reasons similar to why minimum work standards are not necessarily set at the limit that workers will bear before leaving the firm, the optimal contract may not set wages at the minimum acceptable: if part of worker effort is a *gift,* likewise, part of wages paid should be a *gift.*

IV. Reference groups

With the cash posters (or any other work group whose effort is determined not by the work rules but by the group's norms) the question arises: What does the group receive in return for working more than prescribed by the work rules? In the first place the worker may receive leniency in the work rules. Even if the worker habitually works at a speed in excess of work rules, he still benefits from leniency in two ways. First, he derives positive utility from the *gift* by the firm of potential leniency should he slacken his pace; second, as already mentioned, if he has sympathy for other members of the work group, he derives utility from the firm's generous treatment of other members of the group for whom the work rules are a binding constraint. Additionally, the firm may give remuneration in excess of that needed to obtain another worker of similar skills. Thus, excess remuneration and leniency of work rules constitute the major gifts by the firm to its workers.

Presumably, the gift of the worker to the firm, effort in excess of the work rules is linked to the gift of the firm to the worker. Following Mauss and others, reciprocity is a major feature of gift exchange (as also of market exchange).

The *quid pro quo* in gift exchange is, however, established at least slightly differently from market exchange. The norms for effort are established according to the conception of a fair day's work. (Note that Mayo described the work standard in precisely those terms.) In return the workers expect to be treated "fairly" by the firm. The conception of fair treatment has been the subject of considerable work by social psychologists and sociologists. For the most part it is not based on absolute standards, but, rather, on comparison of one's own situation with that of other persons.

According to Festinger [1954], persons have an innate psychological need to compare their actions and treatment with those of others. Persons use comparison with others as a guide to how they ought to behave or how they ought to be treated. The point should be clear to any parent with a young child. Consider the young child who has fallen but not hurt himself/herself. Such situations usually produce that momentary pause before the child decides whether s/he should cry. If the surrounding adults act as if the situation calls for crying, the child is likely to behave accordingly; however, if adults act as if s/he should not cry, the child is likely not to do so. In the context of this paper I wish to note that the child's behavior is not determined by the real phenomenon of being hurt, but rather by the social definition of the situation given by the norms of the surrounding adults. In this way the child calibrates his/her actions by the social standards set by others.[6]

How do people decide that they are fairly treated? There is no natural measure (just as there is no natural language). Merton [1957] has constructed a theory of how people determine the fairness of their treatment by reference to the treatment of reference individuals and treatment of reference groups.

In World War II the Research Branch of the Information and Education Division of the U.S. Department of War conducted a large number of surveys of soldiers' attitudes. Some of these attitudes appear paradoxical from a purely individualistic, utilitarian point of view. For example, in the Army Air Force, in which promotion rates were much higher than in the rest of the army, soldiers were much less satisfied with their chances of promotion than elsewhere. Or, as a second example. although all soldiers abroad showed strong desire

6 For this point of view on social interaction, see Coser [1971] on Park, Mead, and Cooley. The idea of the "definition of the situation" is due to William I. Thomas.

to return to the United States, noncombat soldiers abroad showed little more dissatisfaction with army life than soldiers stationed in the United States. Merton [1957] explains these seemingly paradoxical findings (as well as many others) with the concept of the reference group. The soldier in the Air Force felt unsatisfied with his chances of promotion precisely because the promotion rate was high in the Air Force, thereby enabling him to compare himself with other personnel who had been promoted (and causing him to feel relatively deprived). Noncombat soldiers abroad felt relatively satisfied given their objective conditions because they compared their lot to that of combat soldiers abroad, whereas the soldiers in the United States felt relatively unsatisfied (relative to their objective conditions) because they compared their lot to that of civilians at home. In each of these cases the seemingly paradoxical behavior is quite natural when the soldiers' attitudes are explained in terms of their deprivation relative to that of the appropriate reference group.

At the same time that *The American Soldier* [1949, Volumes 1 and 2] shows how attitudes toward fairness are formed (e.g., through reference to the relative deprivation of the appropriate reference group), it also contains evidence consistent with our hypothesis that *group norms* determine performance (as we have suggested is the case with respect to the cash posters and had been found earlier in the studies by Mayo [1949] and Roethlisberger and Dickson [1947]). In this regard three specific findings are worthy of particular note.

First, the Research Branch chose to measure performance of combat units by the percentage of *nonbattle casualties*. This statistic is equivalent to the percentage of combat men who became ineffective for reasons other than wounds or other battle injuries. This statistic was chosen as the best proxy for the quality of the unit, since it is almost independent of the group's battle environment. It is, as well, unambiguously related to the quality of discipline in the unit: presumably, better organized units would lose smaller fractions of persons outside of battle. An excellent correlation was obtained [Stouffer, 1949, Vol. 2, p. 11] on a company-by-company basis between relatively favorable attitudes toward army life in interviews taken before the Normandy landing and the rate of nonbattle casualties following the Normandy landing in the three tested army divisions. This correlation of performance and attitude is a useful indicator that satisfaction in the job leads to improved job performance, justifying one aspect of our view that the firm will be willing to give a *gift* to the worker to increase his job satisfaction, so as, in turn, to increase his job performance.

There is one other noteworthy statistic from the same study. For one regiment (the Thirty-seventh Regiment of the Ninth Division) a graph was made plotting the percentage of nonbattle casualties of soldiers with and without previous combat experience in the same company. The graph shows a clear relation: in those companies in which the combat veterans had high rates of nonbattle casualties, the new recruits also had high rates (and vice versa). The correlation between the two statistics (taken across companies) was 80 percent [Stouffer, 1949, Vol. 2, p. 27]. This statistic is consistent with the hypothesis that members of a work group tend to take on the *group* norms, the companies with group norms more favorable to army life having fewer casualties among both new recruits and veterans. However, this conclusion follows of necessity only if the Research Branch was correct in its judgment that nonbattle casualties were independent of the environment; otherwise, such a correlation could be obtained because veterans and new recruits respond alike in their nonbattle casualties to changes in the environment.

Finally, there is the study by the Research Branch on the attitudes of soldiers in the Caribbean. It was hypothesized that there would be correlation between dissatisfaction and comfort. Perhaps surprisingly, at least to a very utilitarian view of motivations, the evidence showed at most only weak relation between dissatisfaction and the quality of soldiers' living conditions. This finding is useful in supporting our view that the morale of the working group (and indirectly its norms of work behavior) will depend largely on deprivation relative to that of reference individuals and reference groups, rather than depending on objective conditions alone.

This behavior of the American soldier is exactly consistent with our hypotheses concerning the behavior of the cash posters. We hypothesized (1) that the cash posters worked harder than required because of favorable work attitudes; (2) these attitudes, following Mayo [1949] were not just individual but also attitudes of the work group; (3) these attitudes depended in part upon workers' sense of fair treatment, where fairness was measured by comparison with persons similarly situated. In exact parallel *The American Soldier* shows (1) favorable attitudes were correlated with lower percentages of nonbattle casualties, both on a group-by-group basis and also on an individual basis. (2) The company-by-company correlation between performances of recruits and combat veterans demonstrates that performances were not randomly distributed over individuals but in fact varied systematically over groups. (There is considerable research in social psychology that shows how such patterns occur.) (3) Finally, attitudes of groups of soldiers toward the army can be systematically explained under the hypothesis that soldiers form their attitudes by comparing their situations to that of reference individuals or reference groups. I take the fact that the same model seems to apply to both the cash posters and the American soldier to be an indication of its universality.

V. The fair wage

The gift of the firm to the worker (in return for the worker's gift of hard work for the firm) consists in part of a wage that is fair in terms of the norms of this gift giving. Using reference-individual/reference-group theory, the fairness of this wage depends on how other persons in the worker's reference set are similarly treated. Although persons do sometimes have reference groups, or reference individuals who are dissimilar [Hyman, 1942], in matters of fairness it is probably safe to suppose that most persons compare themselves to persons who are *similar*. In that case one argument of the perceived fairness of the wage will be the wages received by other similar workers. Such workers, of course, include workers who are employed, but workers in the reference set who are unemployed are included as well. While empirically unemployment at any moment affects a fairly small fraction of the labor force, flows in and out of unemployment are large, and most workers have many friends and close relatives. The probability that a whole reference set would be free of unemployment for a significant period (say a year) is not large for most persons.

There is one other argument to the reference wage. To the psychologist or sociologist, to say that persons compare their own behavior or treatment with that in the past is probably neither useful nor profound. But persons certainly do that, and some economic theory (for example, the Modigliani-Duesenberry peak income hypothesis) does depend on such behavior. Thus, one additional argument to the reference wage, in addition to the remuneration of similar employed and unemployed persons and their respective weights in the reference set, is past wages.

Consistent with this observation is the role of past wages in all labor negotiations. Labor disputes often concern the level of past wages, which are the benchmark for current negotiations. To cite a case in point, consider the General Motors strike of 1970. In the 1967–1970 contract wages were indexed, but an eight-cent-per-hour limit was placed on raises due to increases in the cost of living. The cost of living increased relative to wages by considerably more than eight cents per hour with a resultant level of wages twenty-six cents below the fully indexed level [Pearlstine, 1970]. The union claimed that the corporation had already received a windfall gain for the three years of the contract during which period wages were not fully indexed, and the negotiations should concern growth of the real wage from the fully indexed level; the company claimed negotiations should concern growth from the actual 1970 level. This matter was the most contentious issue in the settlement of a long strike.

Summing up all our discussion of the fair wage, the fair wage received by the worker depends on the effort he expends in excess of the work rules, the work rules themselves, the wages of other workers, the benefits of unemployed workers, as well as the number of such workers, and the worker's wages received in previous periods. Our theory of reference-group behavior thus yields a fair wage that looks very much like the wage paid in a Phillips curve:

(5) $\quad w_{i,t+1}^{f} = f(w_{i,t}, w_0, b_u, u, e_i, e_0)$

where

$w_{i,t+1}^{f}$	is the perceived fair wage of individual i at $t + 1$
$w_{i,t}$	is the actual wage of individual i in previous period(s)
w_0	is the wage paid to others in the individual's reference set in current and previous periods
b_u	is unemployment benefits of individuals in the reference set in current and previous periods
u	is the number of unemployed in the reference set in current and previous periods
e_i	is the individual's work rules in current and previous periods
e_0	is the work rules of persons in the individual's reference set in current and previous periods.

Equation (5) is, of course, the basis for a Phillips curve of the traditional sort. It is important to note, however, that contrary to the Phillips relations obtained from search theory [Phelps *et al.*, 1970],

(5) is not derived from market-clearing considerations. In general, there can be workers willing to enter gift relations with a firm, but no firms willing to enter gift relations with the workers. The next two sections model this occurrence. Our models are based upon the preceding discussion of reference groups and of the cash posters.

VI. A model

This section and the next develop formal models that capture to some degree of accuracy most of the gift-giving idea in wage contracts. The ingredients of this model are spelled out in this section as follows.

1. *Norms of effort on the part of workers in the work group.* These norms depend on the work rules of the firm, the average wage paid by the firm, the incentive system of the firm (in terms of the different wages paid for different levels of output or effort), and the utility of co-workers in the firm who are part of the work group and for whom each worker has sympathy. All of these variables are endogenous to the firm. Exogenous to the firm, the norms depend on the returns to other persons in the workers' reference sets. In terms of our model these variables can be summarized by wages received by workers at other firms, the unemployment rate, and unemployment benefits. The model is considerably simplified by assuming only one time period. I do not see that this assumption takes anything away from the argument; it can be easily modified.

We thus summarize norms by the equation,

$$(6) \quad e_n = e_n(\{w(e,\epsilon)\}, e_{\min}, u_1, \ldots, u_J; w_0, u, b_u),$$

where

$\{w(e,\epsilon)\}$ is the function that relates wages of a worker of type ϵ to his effort; this is the remuneration system of the firm

$e_{\min}$ is the work rules

u_j is the utility of the jth worker in the firm

w_0 is the wage paid by other firms (perhaps a vector)

u is the unemployment rate

b_u is the unemployment benefit.

2. *Workers.* Each worker has a utility function. A worker who has been offered employment must decide on his level of effort and whether or not to accept employment at the terms offered. The utility

of each worker depends on the norms for effort, the effort itself, and the wage rate if he is employed; it depends on the unemployment benefit if he is unemployed. A worker makes two choices. If offered employment (i.e., if the firm offers to "exchange gifts"), he must decide whether or not to accept the offer, and, if he accepts, he must decide the size of the reciprocal gift. Thus, a worker of trait ϵ has a utility if working for the firm of

(7) $u(e_n, e, w, \epsilon)$,

and if not working for the firm, of

$u(b_u, \epsilon)$.

If working for the firm, the worker chooses the level of effort e, which maximizes utility u, subject to the condition necessary to maintain his employment; that effort should exceed the firm's minimum requirement, $e \geqq e_{\min}$. Accordingly, the worker chooses a job, if offered, in preference to unemployment accordingly as

(8) $\max_{e \geqq e_{\min}} u(e_n, e, w, \epsilon)$

is greater than or less than

(9) $u(b_u, \epsilon)$.

If a worker has more than one offer from different firms, he chooses the offer that maximizes his utility.

Across workers there is a distribution of tastes ϵ; we call this distribution function $f(\epsilon)$.

3. *Firms.* We are, finally, left with firm behavior. Firms have an output that depends on the work effort of the workers. This output q is

(10) $q = f(e_1, e_2, \ldots, e_J)$,

where J is the number of workers hired. e_j is the effort of worker j.

Firms pay wages in general according to type of worker ϵ and effort, so that $w = w(e, \epsilon)$.

Thus, wage cost is, accordingly,

$$\sum_{j=1}^{J} w(e_j, \epsilon_j),$$

where e_j is the effort of worker j and ϵ_j is the tastes of worker j.

The firm chooses the wage function $w(e, \epsilon)$, work rules, e_{min}, and the number of workers it wishes to hire to maximize profits, which are

$$(11) \quad pf(e_1, \ldots, e_J) - \sum_{j=1}^{J} w(e_j, \epsilon_j),$$

where p is the price of output. The firm's behavior is subject to the constraint that a worker chooses whether or not to join the firm according to whether or not the firm is making the worker his best offer (including unemployment as an alternative); the firm also views e_n as endogenously determined.

Models may differ regarding the firm's knowledge of workers' tastes ϵ; in the models of the next section, where this is relevant, we assume that the probability that it chooses a worker of given tastes ϵ from the unemployment pool is random. That assumption, while convenient, could be modified.

The general model just described of norms-workers-firms is enough taken across all workers and firms to describe aggregate supply for a whole economy. Two such examples are explored in some detail in the next section. These examples describe major features of models with such norm-determined firm-worker interaction.

VII. Two examples

According to the standard neoclassical model of the labor market, the firm purchases labor services in an optimal amount, *given the market wage*. This statement does not completely describe the firm's choice set, although in the *neoclassical* model the inaccuracy is of no importance. The neoclassical firm can purchase all the labor services it wishes if it pays a wage *at least as great as* the market wage. The firm chooses the wage and its purchases of labor services subject to this constraint. If the firm chooses a wage below the market-clearing level, it receives no labor. As far as its choice is concerned, it would be making the same decision if it demanded no labor and paid the market wage; and there is no advantage to choosing a wage in excess of the market rate. The firm's choice of wage therefore is always at the boundary; it will choose the optimal quantity of labor at the market-clearing wage.

However, once labor contracts are viewed in the context of gift exchange, it is not necessarily true that the firm will always choose wages on the boundary. In gift exchange the usual norm is that gifts should be more than the minimum required to keep the other party in the exchange relationship. In terms of the labor market this means that the worker who does no more than necessary to keep his job is the subject of at least some slight loss of reputation; reciprocally, the firm that pays its workers no more than the minimum necessary to retain them will also lose some reputation. In the neoclassical model the firm *never* chooses to pay more than the market-clearing wage because there is no advantage to doing so. In the gift-exchange model, however, the interior solution, in which the firm finds it advantageous to pay a wage in excess of the one at which it can acquire labor, may occur because there are some benefits (as well as costs) from paying a higher wage. Doubtless, this interior solution need not occur. Where it does occur, the labor market is primary. A worker entering the labor market will not automatically find work at the wage received by equally qualified employed persons. If the boundary solution occurs, in contrast, the labor market clears; the market is secondary, and a person in that market can readily obtain work at the wage received by current employees of similar qualifications.

The purpose of this section is to demonstrate by two specific examples the characteristics of the labor market in which gift exchange occurs in the sense that the workers' norm for effort depends upon their treatment by the firm. One example assumes that the firm's work rules are fixed, and with this assumption the equilibrium wage and unemployment are derived. The second example assumes that the real wage is fixed and demonstrates that work rules do not equilibrate supply and demand for labor in the sociological model (with norms) as they do in the neoclassical model. This model is specifically constructed with the behavior of the cash posters in mind.

Example I. Wages

Rather than present a model and show that there will be equilibrium unemployment, we work in reverse. All the parameters and functions of the model are chosen with the exception of the size of the labor force. It is then shown that appropriate particular choice of the size of the labor force will yield an equilibrium with unemployment rate u_0.

Let $\bar{l}$ workers per firm be the supply of labor. $\bar{l}$ will later be chosen to have a particular value to conform to the unemployment rate u_0, but that choice is at the end, not at the beginning of the story.

Let output q be a function of effort e and labor n according to the production function,

(12) $q = (en)^{\alpha}.$

Let effort e of all workers be at the norm e_n. And let all workers be the same so that

(13) $e = e_n.$

Let the effort norm be a function of the wage of the firm relative to the reference wage as

(14) $e_n = -a + b(w/w_r)^{\gamma}, \gamma < 1.$

(Two considerations explain the particular choice of $e_n - w$ function (14). First, the firm chooses w to maximize the number of labor efficiency units per dollar spent. Solow [1979] has shown that such an internal maximum occurs where the elasticity of w with respect to e is equal to unity. And to insure that this choice of w yields the maximum effort per dollar of expenditure, the $e_n - w$ elasticity must be declining. The function (14) has been chosen accordingly with a declining $e_n - w$ elasticity. A second consideration is responsible for the negative intercept of $-a$. If positive effort is obtained at a 0 wage, a 0 wage [with infinite effort per dollar] is optimal.)

Let the reference wage w_r be the geometric mean,

(15) $w_r = w_0^{1-u} b_u^u,$

where

u is the unemployment rate,
w_0 is the wage paid by other firms, and
b_u is the level of unemployment benefits.

Since the firm in question is the typical firm, it also follows that the employment by the firm n is the average number of employed persons per firm, or

(16) $n = (1 - u)\bar{l}.$

Furthermore, again because the firm in question is the typical firm, its wage is the same as the wage of other firms, or

(17) $w = w_0.$

Suppose that u is u_0. It will be shown that with appropriate choice of the parameter $\bar{l} = l_0$, the profit-maximizing firm will choose to hire an amount of labor $n = (1 - u_0)\bar{l}$ if its wage w is the same as the wage of other firms w_0. Consequently, u_0 is an equilibrium rate of unemployment with labor supply l_0.

The firm behaves in the following fashion. With unemployment at $u_0 > 0$, it can obtain all the workers it wants at any wage. Consequently, it chooses n and w to maximize profits, or

(18) $\Pi = (en)^\alpha - wn$

subject to the constraints

(19) $e = e_n$
(20) $e_n = -a + b(w/w_r)^\gamma$
(21) $w_r = w_0^{1-u} b_u^u.$

This maximization problem together with the condition $w = w_0$ yields the demand for labor n^d as a function of the unemployment rate u_0:

(22) $n^d = \left(\alpha^{-1} b_u \left(\dfrac{a\gamma}{1 - \gamma} \right)^{-\alpha} \left(\dfrac{a}{b(1 - \gamma)} \right)^{1/\gamma u_0} \right)^{1/(\alpha - 1)}$

If n^d is consistent with the unemployment rate, then the supply of labor, which is as yet an unchosen parameter of our model, must be

$$(23) \quad \bar{l} = l_0 = \frac{n^d}{1 - u_0} = (1 - u_0)^{-1} \left(\alpha^{-1} b_u \left(\frac{a\gamma}{1 - \gamma} \right)^{-\alpha} \right.$$
$$\left. \times \left(\frac{a}{b(1 - \gamma)} \right)^{1/\gamma u_0} \right)^{1/(\alpha - 1)}$$

With $\bar{l}$ chosen in this fashion according to the right-hand side of (23), our model has an equilibrium at the rate of unemployment u_0, where $0 < u_0 < 1$. Note that the unemployed would be willing to work at the wage paid employed workers, but firms will be unwilling to hire them at that wage, or one which is lower.

Moreover, it is also easy to construct an example in which the firm's choice of w is not interior. After all, if the coefficient $b = 0$ and $a < 0$, the example exactly corresponds to the neoclassical model verbally analyzed at the beginning of this section in which all markets cleared. In our analysis the property, whether or not markets clear, or, alternatively stated, whether labor markets are secondary or primary, is endogenous.[7]

Example 2. Work standards

The first example illustrated the possibility (and the accompanying discussion partially characterized that possibility) that the relation between work norms and wages will cause an economy-wide (or labor-market-wide) equilibrium with nonmarket-clearing prices because firms themselves find it advantageous to set wages above the minimum at which they can freely obtain labor.

Our discussion of the cash posters, however, was not concerned with wages but rather with work rules. According to the standard neoclassical model, even if for some reason wages are not fixed at market-clearing levels, still firms should adjust work rules to the point where supply and demand for labor are equal *(even at a non-*

---

7 Just because some markets clear does not mean that there is no unemployment. Unemployed workers may be waiting for an opportunity to take a primary sector job. See Hall [1975].

equilibrial wage). This section gives an example, in which the work rules will not equilibrate labor supply and demand. It is not the simplest example – partly because of our desire to make the model a faithful representation of the cash posters, and partially also because the reaction of workers to norms inherently involves a great deal of behavior that cannot easily be represented by simple linear functions.

Because in the standard neoclassical model work standards would equate demand and supply for labor even at a fixed nonequilibrating wage rate, we start with the assumption that the wage rate $\overline{w}$ is fixed. Although artificial, we could assume that the government has controlled wages. Certainly this occasionally happens when the government imposes certain forms of incomes policy.

Recall that among the cash posters some workers worked much above the work standard set by the firm (45 percent for Granara and Murphy) while some workers were quite close to the margin (only 2 percent above for Burke and Donovan).

To represent a model in which some workers are above the margin while other workers are at the margin, it is necessary to have at least two types of workers. For that reason our model has two groups of workers with different tastes. Poor workers form a fraction p of the work force. Good workers form a fraction $1 - p$.

In the story behind our model the firm is capable of identifying the tastes of workers only after they have joined the firm, but not before. In terms of the cash posters, who could have predicted that the almost equally outgoing and gregarious Murphy and Burke would have work records which were polar opposites? Homans hints that this difference may have occurred in part because Burke socialized primarily with a group of "ledger posters," while the rest of the cash posters socialized mainly among themselves. Certainly no personnel officer could have predicted such an occurrence.

Although the firm can measure performance easily once workers are hired, it is assumed that it cannot fire them without a reduction in the work norms. As a result, in the model constructed labor effort is observable ex post but not predictable ex ante.

Worker behavior. Among the two types of workers, good workers who work for the firm have utility, denoted U^+, where

$$(24) \quad U^+ = A - B(e - (e_n + \epsilon))^2.$$

The parameter A depends on wages, but since they are assumed fixed, we have suppressed that dependency. Poor workers who work for the firm have utility, denoted U^-, where

(25) $\quad U^- = A - B(e - (e_n - \epsilon))^2.$

The parameters A and B are both positive, e_n is the norm of work effort, e is actual effort by the individual worker, and ϵ is a parameter reflecting the type of worker. U^+ and U^- are the utilities of good workers and bad workers, respectively, when working for the firm. Workers have the option of working for the firm with effort e and also the option of quitting and being unemployed. In that case their utility is assumed to be 0.

A worker who works for a firm maximizes his utility subject to abiding by the work rules of the firm. Thus, a good worker with utility function U^+ chooses e to maximize

(26) $\quad A - B(e - (e_n + \epsilon))^2,$

subject to the constraint

(27) $\quad e \geqq e_{\min}^+,$

where $e_{\min}^+$ is the minimum work standard set by the firm for good workers. Accordingly, for such a worker if U^+ working for the firm is positive, the worker chooses to work with effort e^+:

(28) $\quad e^+ = \max(e_{\min}^+, e_n + \epsilon).$

Similarly, if U^- working for the firm is positive, a poor worker chooses to work with effort e^-:

(29) $\quad e^- = \max(e_{\min}^-, e_n - \epsilon).$

Norms.   The norms of behavior depend upon the work rules,

(30) $\quad e_n = e_n(e_{\min}^-, e_{\min}^+).$

Later it will be assumed that $e_{\min}^-$ and $e_{\min}^+$ have an effect on norms only insofar as they are a binding constraint on workers' effort.

Firm behavior. On its side, the firm takes into account the reaction of the workers' effort to the norms and the reaction of the norms to work rules. In the case of excess supply of labor, where labor is freely available as long as U^+ and U^- are positive, the firm chooses e_{min}^+, e_{min}^-, and n to maximize profits, or

$$(31) \quad (\bar{e}(e_{min}^-, e_{min}^+)n)^\alpha - \bar{w}n,$$

where $\bar{e}(\ )$ is the function combining (28), (29), and (30) with the appropriate weights to account for the dependence of average effort on work rules.

Accordingly, at an interior maximum the firm that can obtain all the labor it wishes will choose e_{min}^- and e_{min}^+ to maximize $\bar{e}(e_{min}^-, e_{min}^+)$, and its demand for labor according to the marginal product condition,

$$(32) \quad \alpha\bar{e}(e_{min}^{-*}, e_{min}^{+*})^\alpha n^{\alpha-1} = \bar{w}.$$

As long as n so chosen by the typical firm is less than $\bar{l}$, the demand for labor is less than the supply, and the assumption that the firm can obtain all the labor it wishes is justified.

Problems with obtaining an interior maximum. The question, however, arises, how there can be an interior maximum for e_{min}^+ or e_{min}^-. After all, why should the firm not increase e_{min}^+ just up to the point where all good workers are on the verge of quitting? (In so doing, it also may have the added dividend of screening out the poorer workers.) In the real world workers usually apply sanctions against such behavior by the firm. For example, in the case of the cash posters, remember that Homans recorded a work slowdown in a previous dispute with a supervisor. In our model this is represented by the fact that as the work rules force workers to work sufficiently in excess of the norms, they quit.

Let the fraction p of poor workers be ½. Let the tastes parameter ϵ be 1. And let the parameters A and B in (24) and (25) be 2 and ½, respectively, so that

$$(33) \quad U^+ = 2 - \tfrac{1}{2}(e - (e_n + \epsilon))^2$$
$$(34) \quad U^- = 2 - \tfrac{1}{2}(e - (e_n - \epsilon))^2.$$

Good workers, who maximize U^+, will choose

(35) $e = e_n + \epsilon$

as long as they are unconstrained by the work rules. Similarly, if unconstrained, poor workers, who maximize U^-, will choose

(36) $e = e_n - \epsilon$.

We assume that the work rules have an effect on the effort norm if and only if they are binding. Accordingly, the norm depends on $\max(e^+_{min} - (e_n + \epsilon),0)$ and $\max(e^-_{min} - (e_n - \epsilon),0)$. Furthermore, it is assumed that the norms are egalitarian in that a difference between the work rules for the two types of workers will have a negative effect on the norms.

Accordingly, the norm in this example follows the formula,

$$(37)   e_n = 6 - 0.8 \max(e^+_{min} - (e_n + \epsilon),e^-_{min} - (e_n - \epsilon),0) - 20\,|e^+_{min} - e^-_{min}|.$$

The second term of (37) reflects the decline in the norm of effort as the work rules become increasingly binding on the workers' choice of effort. The third term reflects the effect on the norm of an inequality in the treatment of the two types of workers.

It is easy to check that the firm which wishes to maximize $\bar{e}$ will choose

(38) $e^+_{min} = e^-_{min} \leqq 5$,

and at this maximum $\bar{e} = 6$.

I will sketch the proof. First, inequality in e^+_{min} and e^-_{min} causes such a large reduction in e_n (the coefficient of the last term of (37) being 20) that the firm always finds it advantageous to set $e^+_{min} = e^-_{min}$. In that case the formula for e_n (37) can be simplified to

(39) $e_n = 6 - 0.8 \max(e_{min} - (e_n - \epsilon),0)$.

A bit of algebra shows that with $\epsilon = 1$ (39) can be rewritten as

(40A) $e_n = 6$ $e_{min} \leqq 5$
(40B) $e_n = 30 - 4e_{min} - 4$ $e_{min} \geqq 5$.

It is easy to check using (34), (40A), (40B) and the value of $\epsilon = 1$ that U^- is positive if $e_{min} < 5.4$ and negative if $e_{min} > 5.4$. Similarly, U^+ is positive if $e_{min} < 5.8$ and is negative for $e_{min} > 5.8$.

Thus, in the range $0 \leqq e_{min} < 5.4$ both good and bad workers are working. For $0 \leqq e_{min} \leqq 5$ work rules are binding on neither good nor bad workers, and therefore

$$(41) \quad \bar{e} = \frac{1}{2}(e_n + \epsilon) + \frac{1}{2}(e_n - \epsilon) = e_n = 6, 0 \leqq e_{min} \leqq 5.$$

For $5 < e_{min} < 5.4$ work rules are binding on poor workers but not on good workers. U^- and U^+ are both positive so both good and bad workers are at work. Hence

$$(42) \quad \bar{e} = \frac{1}{2}(e_n + \epsilon) + \frac{1}{2}e_{min} \qquad 5 < e_{min} < 5.4$$
$$(43) \quad\;\; = 13.5 - 1.5e_{min} < 6 \qquad 5 < e_{min} < 5.4.$$

By design of the example, for $e_{min} < 5.4$ U^- is negative; also by (40B) for $e_{min} > 5.4$, $e_n + \epsilon < e_{min}$, so work rules are binding on good workers. U^+ is positive for $e_{min} < 5.8$. Consequently, in the range $5.4 < e_{min} < 5.8$ only good workers are at work, and since their effort is constrained by work rules,

$$(44) \quad \bar{e} = e_{min} \qquad 5.4 < e_{min} < 5.8.$$

For $e_{min} > 5.8$ $\bar{e}$ is indeterminate, since U^+ and U^- are both negative. The number of workers willing to work is, however, 0. Hence $\bar{e}$ is maximized according to (41), (43), and (44) at $\bar{e} = 6$ with $e_{min}^+ = e_{min}^- \leqq 5$.

To obtain an example with unemployment rate u_0, it is only necessary to choose $\bar{l} = l_0$ consistent with u_0 and the marginal productivity condition for labor demand so that

$$(45) \quad \bar{l} = l_0 = (1 - u_0)^{-1} (\alpha^{-1} 6^{-\alpha} \overline{w})^{1/(\alpha-1)}.$$

Remark. This example corresponds exactly to cash poster behavior. The firm paid the same wage to all workers. One group of workers (a minority) worked at the work standard, or very close to it. Other workers worked above that standard. For reasons unspecified by Homans, but which are consistent with our model, the firm did not raise standards on either good workers or poor workers. At the equilibrium unemployment is involuntary.

VIII. Conclusion

This paper has explored the idea that labor contracts are partial gift exchanges. According to this idea, at least in part, wages are determined by, and in turn also influence, the norms of workers' effort; similarly, workers' effort is determined, at least in part, by these norms. A relation between the terms of exchange and norms is in our view what differentiates gift exchange from pure market exchange.

Indeed, while the norms may be greatly influenced by the same things as market prices, there is still a major difference between pure market exchange and gift exchange. In pure market exchange the maximum price at which a buyer is willing to purchase a commodity or factor service is the minimum at which the respective commodity or factor service is obtainable. Obversely, the minimum price at which a seller is willing to sell a commodity or factor service is the maximum at which the respective commodity or factor service can be sold. In gift exchange buyers may be willing to pay more than the minimum at which they can purchase a commodity or factor service because of the effect of the terms of exchange on the norms. Similarly, sellers may be willing to accept less than the maximum at which they can sell a commodity or factor service because of the effects of the terms of exchange on the norms. It has been shown that due to this behavior with gift exchange markets need not clear. Thus, the gift-exchange economy and the neoclassical economy differ in at least one fundamental respect. Future papers will explore further differences between the two models of exchange.

University of California, Berkeley

References

Azariadis, C., "Implicit Contracts and Unemployment Equilibria," *Journal of Political Economy,* LXXXIII (Dec. 1975), 1183–1202.

Baily, M. N., "Wages and Employment Under Uncertain Demand," *Review of Economic Studies,* XLI (Jan. 1974), 37–50.

Belshaw, C. S., *Traditional Exchange and Modern Markets* (Englewood Cliffs, NJ: Prentice-Hall, 1965).

Coser, L. A., *Masters of Sociological Thought: Ideas in Historical and Social Context* (New York: Harcourt Brace Jovanovich, 1971).

Doeringer, P. B., and M. J. Piore, *Internal Labor Markets and Manpower Analysis* (Lexington, MA: D. C. Heath & Co., 1971).

Edwards, R., *Contested Terrain: The Transformation of the Workplace in the Twentieth Century* (New York: Basic Books, 1979).

Etzioni, A. W., *Modern Organizations* (Englewood Cliffs, NJ: Prentice-Hall, 1971).

Festinger, L., "A Theory of Social Comparison Processes," *Human Relations,* VII (1954), 117–40; reprinted in *Readings in Reference Group Therapy,* Herbert H. Hyman and Eleanor Singer, eds. (New York: The Free Press, 1968).

Freeman, R. L., and J. L. Medoff, "The Two Faces of Unionism," *The Public Interest,* No. 57 (Fall 1979), 69–93.

Hall, R. E., "The Rigidity of Wages and the Persistence of Unemployment," *Brookings Papers on Economic Activity,* III (1975), 301–49.

Hirschman, A. O., *Exit, Voice and Loyalty* (Cambridge, MA: Harvard University Press, 1970).

Homans, G. C., "Status Among Clerical Workers," *Human Organization,* XII (Spring 1953), 5–10; reprinted in G. C. Homans, *Sentiments and Activities* (New York: Free Press of Glencoe, 1962).

"The Cash Posters," *American Sociological Review,* XIX (Dec. 1954), 724–33; reprinted in G. C. Homans, *Sentiments and Activities* (New York: Free Press of Glencoe, 1962).

Hyman, H. H., "The Psychology of Status," *Archives of Psychology,* No. 269 (1942); reprinted in part in *Readings in Reference Group Theory,* Herbert H. Hyman and Eleanor Singer, eds. (New York: The Free Press, 1968).

Leibenstein, H., *Beyond Economic Man: A New Foundation for Microeconomics* (Cambridge, MA: Harvard University Press, 1976).

Mauss, M., *The Gift: Forms and Functions of Exchange in Archaic Societies,* translated by Ian Cunnison (London: Cohen and West, 1954).

Mayo, E., *The Social Problems of an Industrial Civilization* (London: Routledge and Kegan Paul, 1949).

Merton. R. K., *Social Theory and Social Structure,* revised and enlarged edition (Glencoe, IL: The Free Press, 1957).

Okun, A., "Inflation: Its Mechanics and Welfare Costs," *Brookings Papers on Economic Activity,* II (1975), 366–73.

Prices and Quantities: A Macroeconomic Analysis (Washington, D.C.: The Brookings Institution, 1981).

Pearlstine, N., "Auto Pact Tension Eases; Strike Chances Viewed as Tied to Chrysler, GM Parleys," *Wall Street Journal,* CLXXVI, No. 48 (Sept. 4, 1970), 5, column 2.

Phelps, E. S. *et al., The Microeconomic Foundations of Employment and Inflation Theory* (New York: Norton, 1970).

Roethlisberger, F. J., and W. J. Dickson, *Management and the Worker: An Account of a Research Program Conducted by the Western Electric Company, Hawthorne Works, Chicago* (Cambridge, MA: Harvard University Press, 1947).

Solow, R. H., "Another Possible Source of Wage Stickiness," *Journal of Macroeconomics*, I (Winter 1979), 79–82.

"On Theories of Unemployment," *American Economic Review*, LXX (March 1980), 1–10.

Stoft, S., "Cheat-Threat Theory," University of California Thesis Prospectus, August 1980.

Stouffer, S. A., E. A. Suchman, L. C. de Vinney, S. A. Star, and R. M. Williams, Jr., *The American Soldier: Adjustment During Army Life*, Vol. 1 (Princeton, NJ: Princeton University Press, 1949).

Stouffer, S. A., A. A. Lumsdaine, M. H. Lumsdaine, R. M. Williams, Jr., M. B. Smith, I. L. Jarvis, S. A. Star, and L. S. Cottrell, Jr., *The American Soldier: Combat and its Aftermath*, Vol. 2 (Princeton, NJ: Princeton University Press, 1949).

Titmuss, R. M., *The Gift Relationship: From Human Blood to Social Policy* (New York: Random House, 1971).

9
Loyalty filters

When people go through experiences, frequently their loyalties, or their values, change. I call these value-changing experiences "loyalty filters." This paper considers the case where these values are partially, but not totally, changeable. In addition, persons, by having a choice over their experiences, can exercise some choice over their values; or perhaps more typically, persons may choose for their children experiences that will lead them to have desired values. Insofar as this occurs, values are not fixed, as in standard economics, but are a matter of choice. Economic theory, which is largely a theory of choice, then becomes a useful tool in analyzing how these values are chosen. Most persons attempt to choose values for their children (and perhaps also for themselves) according to their economic opportunities that allow them to get along economically. According to Robert Coles' *Children of Crisis,* not only the wealthy (who will be discussed at some length in Section II), but also the poorest of the poor – immigrants, sharecroppers, and mountaineers – consciously teach their children values aimed at leading them best to survive economically.

The Wealth of Nations concerned itself with the issue of how the economy would behave if everyone were to behave selfishly. Adam Smith's famous answer to this question in terms of the invisible hand is the key result in economic theory. Since the time of Edgeworth (see Amartya Sen, 1977, p. 317), it has been fashionable for non-Marxist economic theorists to follow Smith's presumed worst case assumption – that all persons are totally selfish. Yet as Sen points out, this assumption is made for reasons of convenience, not because economists empirically assume that all persons act only out of selfishness.

This paper will explore the extent to which parents interested only

University of California-Berkeley. I thank Donald Hayes, Hajime Miyazaki, and Janet Yellen for invaluable help and comments, and the Institute of Business and Economic Research, University of California-Berkeley, for logistical support. I also thank the National Science Foundation for financial support under research grant no. SES-8119150.

in their children's economic welfare will teach them to be totally selfish. Section I gives an example in which children are taught to be honest, even to their own detriment. Such a teaching may cause children to act against their own short-run interest even while it serves their long-run economic interests. Similarly, Section II yields a model where children are taught to be loyal to their class interests; this teaching may not serve their individual short-run interest, but it does serve their individual long-run interest. Each of these models is motivated by an empirical observation. In the case of Section I, this observation concerns the economic well-being of the high-minded Quakers: if selfishness pays off, why should the Quakers do so well? Section II is motivated by Coles' studies of the way in which privileged children learn to view those less fortunate as "others," in contrast to "us."

The models of Sections I and II are meant to show economic man as not being undeviatingly selfish. In Section I, he is undeviatingly honest, even against his interest, and in Section II he is undeviatingly loyal to his class interest. Yet at the same time his long-run interests have been maximized by teaching him a code of conduct that leads him, insofar as possible, to act in his best long-run interest. Section III continues the process of making economic man less undeviatingly selfish. This section concerns economic and political elites who are the products of consciously styled elite academies. Examples of such elites come from military service academies, prestige universities, and other institutions that not only give technical training, but also teach loyalty to these institutions and the type of persons who are their faculty or alumni. Where these institutions are aligned with the government (or else where their graduates have other monopoly powers), it is shown that the curriculum that best serves its alumni not only teaches technical skills, but also loyalty to the type of person who is a fellow graduate. In the model of this section, the elite graduate is unselfish in serving his country; nevertheless, due to the biases in his values, the interests of the elite end up being served, as well perhaps as the interest of the country. The picture emerges of well-trained, well-meaning civil servants who act selflessly according to their best conscience, yet nevertheless manage to earn more than the competitive wage due to the cultural biases that have been chosen.

Finally, before getting into the specific models, I would like to make a few remarks. Albert Hirschman's *Exit, Voice and Loyalty*

(1970) is the only recent non-Marxist economics to emphasize the role of loyalty in economic theory.[1] Yet, for the most part, his book is unconcerned with how loyalties begin, which is the focus of this paper. I resisted the temptation to call this paper "Entrance, Voice, and Loyalty," which would have emphasized the contrast with Hirschman's work, because the title "Loyalty Filters" better conveys the generality of my subject matter. In this regard, I would like to remark on the particular and illustrative nature of the examples that follow. They fail in their particularity to reflect the many important possible types of loyalty filter. The agent who experiences the filter may consciously or unconsciously choose the experience. He may be conscious or unconscious of the effect of the experience on his loyalties. And the experience may not only be chosen by himself (or an agent such as his parents acting on his behalf), but instead by another agent acting in his own selfish interest, such as an advertiser interested in fostering brand loyalty to the product he sells, or an employer interested in extracting unselfish performances from his employees.[2] Furthermore, according to George Homans (1950), loyalties change according to almost every role a person plays and almost every situation that involves him. The preceding rudimentary classification of loyalty filters according to choice/consciousness/agent choosing/role of agent should alert us to the great variety of loyalty filters. The examples given below are meant as an illustrative teaching device and as an invitation to the reader to roll his own examples of loyalty filters.

1 In Marxist terminology, this paper concerns how a class 'in itself' becomes a class "for itself" (Anthony Giddens, 1975, p. 30). The prediction following Marx that most poverty stricken in society will be reactionary in attitude (Giddens, p. 37) accords exactly with that of the model of class loyalty in Section II. Only extra-economic attitudes will cause the poor to unite in their own class interests according to that model. That prediction is also consistent with the observation that most socialist revolutions have occurred in the wake of wars fought for reasons only incidental to the socialist takeover which later occurs.

2 A very different type of loyalty filter from those in this paper is analyzed by myself and William Dickens (1982). I would like to record my debt to him for what I learned while jointly writing that paper.

I. A model of honesty and cooperative behavior

A. Motivation

As mentioned above, the model in this section is motivated by the assumption of selfishness in economic models. It is also motivated by an experiment in social psychology (Fred Arnstein and Kenneth Feigenbaum, 1967). In this experiment, persons of different religious persuasions were asked to play a game of the prisoner's dilemma variety; in this game, noncooperative behavior improved considerably the lot of the noncooperative player provided the other players' behavior remained cooperative. Conversely, cooperative players fared quite poorly if the other players were noncooperative. It turned out that the Quakers, as might be expected, ranked quite high in terms of the trustfulness and cooperation of their responses, but low in terms of their economic rationality. This result is curious because in real life, Quakers are usually considered one of the wealthiest minority groups in the United States (Gordon Allport, 1958, p. 72). The model below is intended, accordingly, to show that honesty and cooperative behavior pay off; the honest person is not just a systematic "sucker."

The model is quite trivial; it corresponds exactly to a known observation: couriers who carry large sums of money are often "bonded." Apparently, it pays to bond such persons, which in effect is to guarantee their honesty. According to the model here, it pays persons to bond themselves by acquiring traits that cause them to appear honest. And the cheapest way to acquire such traits according to our model is, in fact, to be honest! This distinction between *appearance* and *actuality* of honesty has been discussed by Max Weber (1958).[3]

---

3 The coincidence between Weber's view and that of this paper regarding honesty can be seen in the following discussion of Benjamin Franklin by Weber:

> Now all Franklin's moral attitudes are coloured with utilitarianism. Honesty is useful, because it assures credit; so are punctuality, industry, frugality, and that is the reason they are virtues. A logical deduction from this would be that where, for instance, the appearance of honesty serves the same purpose that would suffice, and an unnecessary surplus of this virtue would evidently appear to Franklin's eyes as unproductive waste. . . . But in fact the matter is not by any means so simple. Benjamin Franklin's own character, as it appears in the unusual candidness of his autobiography, belies that suspicion. The

Weber's essays on the Protestant ethic are the classic description of how different experiences result in different personality types, with important economic consequences.

B. The model

The nature of jobs (from which labor demand is derived). Let there be only one type of job in the economy and let this job have a product y. Workers in this job, however, have an opportunity to embezzle an amount x with probability q unless there is surveillance. It would be straightforward to let there be surveillance costs, but complication is avoided by assuming these costs to be prohibitive.

The nature of workers (from which labor supply is derived). The utility of a worker depends on his income according to the utility function $u(\cdot)$. Parents wish to maximize their children's welfare. They can train their children to be dishonest, which in this model means to embezzle whenever they can get away with it; or they can train their children to be honest.

Equilibrium wages of dishonest workers. Employers are not fooled about the characters of their employees. A dishonest worker will be seen as such and his wage will be reduced by his expected embezzlement. Assuming risk-neutral competitive employers, a dishonest worker will receive a wage of $y - qx$, which is his product net of his expected embezzlement. Remember, however, that the worker has a chance to embezzle x with probability q. Thus with chance $(1 - q)$, the dishonest worker has utility $u(y - qx)$, and with chance q, he has utility $u(y - qx + x)$. The net result is an expected utility given by

$$(1) \quad E(u) = (1 - q)u(y - qx) + qu(y + (1 - q)x).$$

circumstance that he ascribes his recognition of the utility of virtue to a divine revelation which was intended to lead him in the path of righteousness shows that something more than mere garnishing for purely egocentric motives is involved. [pp. 52–53]

In the view of this paper, Franklin, no matter how utilitarian his beliefs, could not acquire the appearance of honesty without its actuality.

Equilibrium wage of honest workers.   Alternatively, according to the model, parents may train their children to be honest. Such training may require a cost to the parents, which we assume to be paid by the children. We call this cost c_h. Employers will pay honest persons their product y, so that their income net of training costs is $y - c_h$, and their utility is $u(y - c_h)$. Parents interested in maximizing their children's welfare will choose to make their children honest provided

$$(2)\quad u(y - c_h) > (1 - q)u(y - qx) + qu(y + (1 - q)x).$$

This last inequality always holds for given q, y, and x, provided c_h is sufficiently small and u has diminishing returns.

Very dishonest behavior.   There is a final question. Children could presumably also be taught to act honest yet embezzle when they get a chance. I will assume that such training is quite costly. Suppose the cost of such training is c_{vd} (*vd* for very dishonest) and $c_{vd} - c_h > qx$. In this case, the costs of such training exceed the gains from dishonesty qx, so that it never pays parents to train their children in this way. It may appear at first glance that it should not be difficult to teach people to dissemble their values. But persons often have a hard time hiding their true nature. The rareness of acting talent can be perceived any day of the week by a comparison of daytime and nighttime TV.

Furthermore, there is evidence that traits once acquired (in this case, honesty) are often difficult to lose even when they have become dysfunctional. Robert Merton describes how bureaucrats' "adherence to the rules, originally conceived as a means, becomes transformed into an end-in-itself" (1956, p. 253). In my model of childrearing, honesty may begin as a means for economic betterment, but then there is a displacement of goals so that the person so trained will refrain from embezzlement where there is no penalty. Psychological experiments with animals show similarly that animals may quite easily be trained to have dysfunctional behavior. See, for example, Henry Gleitman's example (1981, p. 148) of trained helplessness in dogs.

Remarks.   The role of jointness of production in training in this model should be noted. It is assumed that at the cost c_h, parents can train their children to *appear* honest. But to make children appear honest, it is easiest to make them also *be* honest. There is a return to *appearing* honest, but not to *being* honest. It pays parents to teach their children to be honest because the individually functional trait of appearing honest is jointly produced with the individually dysfunctional trait of being honest.

It should also be noted that the word *embezzlement* need not be taken too literally. Any form of noncooperative behavior by workers, which the firm will find expensive and difficult to police, can play the exact same role as embezzlement. In many jobs, workers are given considerable scope for lack of cooperation before there will be retaliation by their supervisor. (See my 1982 article for an earlier discussion.) Such lack of cooperation has consequences similar to embezzlement in the model which has been presented. In the next section, a very similar model is proposed; embezzlement, however, is replaced by the more general concept of noncooperation.

II. Class loyalty

This section concerns a theory of class loyalty and its formation. Although individualistic economic theory is based upon the assumption that individuals act selfishly out of their own interests, it is certainly empirically and theoretically possible that persons are loyal to other ideals. Coles' *Privileged Ones* describes how wealthy children think about poorer persons. The model in this section is motivated by his study.

A. Studies of social identification (Coles, Allport)

Coles' books, which are the result of fifteen years' intensive work by a trained child psychologist, may be the most complete and detailed study ever made of the formation of class loyalties. Nevertheless, the whole process whereby the socialization occurs is still a bit mysterious, even from Coles' detailed accounts. Why this mystery is of necessity the case is explained by Allport in his discussion of the learning of social values via identification of children with their parents:

> Learning through identification seems basically to involve a type of muscle strain or postural imitation. Supposing the child, hypersensitive to parental cues, senses a tightness or rigidity when his

parents are talking about the Italian family that has moved in next door. In the very act of perceiving these parental cues, the child grows tight and rigid. . . . After this associated experience, he may tend, ever so slightly, to feel a tenseness (an incipient anxiety) whenever he hears (or thinks) of Italians. The process is infinitely subtle. [1958, pp. 278–79]

Despite this subtlety, because of the intensity of his study, Coles is able to report, here and there, the emergence of social values among the wealthy as the younger children in his sample ask their mommy or daddy embarrassing questions such as why their family should not share their wealth with others. There are many answers to these questions, such as "Daddy works hard for what he earns"; "Mommy and Daddy give a great deal to charity"; "there are so many poor persons our contribution could only be very small." In some cases, the questions persist, particularly where the children identify with the maid and possibly also with her children. However, in these cases of persistence, these questions are usually abandoned when mommy (typically) makes it clear that it is not nice to annoy the loving daddy with such annoying and persistent questions. The children then re-immerse themselves in leading the "busy, busy lives" (Coles' phrase) which their parents have planned for them.

Although much of the process of socialization is difficult to see, it is clear that it is quite intentional on the part of these wealthy parents that their children are taught to view themselves as "different" from those who are less fortunate. This does not mean, typically, that "others" are to be despised; but almost all the wealthy children in Coles' book have a sense of identification with "us," children and families who are equally well to do, in contrast to "others" who are less fortunate.

The role of the difference in the lives of rich children and poor children in causing this sense of distinction and identification is made clear in the description of a young New Orleans girl at the time of the racial trouble in the early 1960's. I wish to stress, as does Coles, that the social meanings ascribed by this girl, although seen through the eyes of a child, are, nevertheless, exactly those intended by her parents. According to Coles, " 'Our maid's children don't know about finger bowls,' a seven-year-old New Orleans girl says. She also says – the year is 1960 – that 'the kids going into those [desegregated] schools don't know about finger bowls either; and they don't know how to smile and say thank-you to the people in the mobs'" (1977, p. 530).

The girl's plan of action for the black children going into the desegregated schools is to be unfailingly polite (i.e., to learn about finger bowls). This plan of action and the statement I have quoted are explained by Coles as correctly perceiving the role of manners in differentiating the wealthy from the poor. Displaying such politeness, in the view of the child, the black children will achieve her own status (and that of her family) and the mobs will cease to be hostile.

To summarize, wealthy parents tend to teach their children an identification with other persons of wealth and to view the less fortunate as others. Furthermore, this teaching is quite intentional, either learned through certain coded messages such as "manners" inherent in the way of life of the wealthy, in subtle demonstrations of annoyance or tension by parents, or, finally, occasionally, but except in rare cases only to younger children, by requests not to annoy mommy or daddy with needless questions. This section will construct a model wherein parents interested in maximizing their children's economic welfare will teach them such values. According to the technology, parents may teach their children to have such class values, but such values, as in the earlier model of honesty, cannot be dissembled. Thus persons cannot pretend to identify with other members of their class without actually being loyal.

B. A model

The model will be quite similar to the one in the last section, only with some added generality. Let there be two types of persons, the wealthy, represented by W, and the poor, represented by P. Suppose that a W may be hired either by a P or a W, and that a W will have a marginal product, if cooperative, in a job provided by a W of y_{WW} and will have a chance of engaging in noncooperative behavior that will reduce this marginal product by x_{WW} with probability q_{WW}. The double subscript WW indicates that a W (the first subscript) is providing a job to a W (the second subscript). The probability that a W so hired will engage in noncooperative behavior will depend on his class loyalties. If loyal to the W, his probability of noncooperative behavior will be low; if loyal to the P, his probability of noncooperative behavior in such a job will be high. Again, as in the previous model, and again only for modeling convenience, assume that surveillance is not possible.

In the usual neoclassical model, contracts may be made between any two persons. Assume, therefore, similarly and symmetrically with the WW case, that a P may also hire a W. The marginal product of a W working for a P is y_{PW} with a chance of noncooperative behavior q_{PW} with cost to the employer of x_{PW}.

Consistent with the notation of the earlier model, the cost of instilling class loyalties is denoted by the letter c, with c_{WW} the cost of instilling loyalty of a W to the W and c_{PW} the cost of instilling loyalties of a W to the P.

The individual person maximizes his utility. This utility depends on his income and also on his behavior on the job, which may be cooperative or noncooperative. The individual benefits from noncooperative behavior, but it is not automatic that such behavior that costs the employer x_{WW} or x_{PW} will result in a benefit to the employee of equal amount. I will assume that the individual values the returns from noncooperative behavior at a fraction α, $0 \leqq \alpha \leqq 1$, of its cost. As before, let the individual have a utility function $u(\cdot)$, which in this case depends on the wage plus the value to him of being noncooperative, if he chooses that mode of behavior.

The individual has three choices: whether to work for a W or a P; whether to be loyal to the W or not; whether to be loyal to the P or not. In general, a person with a chance of noncooperation q at cost x in a job with cooperative product y, and with loyalties that are acquired at cost c, will receive a wage $y - qx$ and therefore have an expected utility

$$(3) \quad E(u) = (1 - q)u(y - qx - c) + qu(y - qx + \alpha x - c).$$

Adoption of the following notation allows a single expression for the maximization problem of a W. Let e_{WW} be a dummy variable equal to unity if W is employed by a W, and equal to zero otherwise; let l_{WW} be a dummy variable equal to unity if W is loyal to the W, and equal to zero otherwise; and let l_{PW} be a dummy variable, similarly, equal to unity if W is loyal to the P and equal to zero otherwise.

Accordingly, a W chooses for himself (or for his child) the variables e_{WW}, l_{WW}, l_{PW} to maximize $E(u)$, which is given by the expression

$$(4) \quad E(u) = e_{WW}E_{WW}(u) + (1 - e_{WW})E_{PW}(u),$$

where $E_{WW}(u)$ and $E_{PW}(u)$ are the expected utilities of a W working for a W and a P, respectively. (An explicit expression for $E(u)$ can be derived as a function of e_{WW}, l_{WW}, and l_{PW} by use of (3). Let E_{WW} and E_{PW} be written as functions of l_{WW} and l_{PW} by insertion into (3) of the appropriate subscripts on $E(u)$, q, y, x, and c, with q_{WW} and q_{PW} each an explicit function of its two arguments, l_{WW} and l_{PW}. Substitution of the expressions for E_{WW} and E_{PW} into (4) yields $E(u)$ as a function of the three optimizing variables, e_{WW}, l_{WW}, and l_{PW}.)

Assume that there are K_W units of capital owned by the W and K_P units of capital owned by the poor, and that both types of capital use both W and P labor with constant returns to scale. Then in equilibrium $E_{WW}(u) = E_{PW}(u)$, or, in words, the expected utility of a W working for a W and for a P are equal. The number of W working for W-capital and the number of W working for P-capital will be proportional to K_W and K_P respectively; thus the fraction of W working for W is $K_W/(K_P + K_W)$.[4]

In equilibrium, a W is indifferent to working for a W or a P, but if working for a W, the maximizer will choose loyalties to the W and not to the P; if working for the P, the opposite choices will be made, provided c_{WW} and c_{PW} are sufficiently small.

A W working for a W will receive expected utility which can be expressed (with appropriate use of subscripts in (3) as

$$
\begin{aligned}
(5) \quad & (1 - q_{WW}(l_{WW}, l_{PW})) \, u(y_{WW} - q_{WW}(l_{WW}, l_{PW}) x_{WW} \\
& - l_{WW} c_{WW} - l_{PW} c_{PW}) + q_{WW}(l_{WW}, l_{PW}) \, u(y_{WW} \\
& - (q_{WW}(l_{WW}, l_{PW}) - \alpha) x_{WW} - l_{WW} c_{WW} - l_{PW} c_{PW}).
\end{aligned}
$$

Equation (5) is maximized (provided c_{WW} is sufficiently small, and given the assumptions that q_{WW} decreases with l_{WW} and increases

---

4 This intuitive result depends upon various assumptions in addition to constant returns to scale. The production functions with W and P owners of capital must be the same. In addition the following symmetry conditions are required: $q_{WW}(x, y) = q_{PW}(y, x)$, $q_{WP}(x, y) = q_{PP}(y, x)$, $x_{WW} = x_{PW}$, $x_{PP} = x_{WP}$, $c_{WW} = c_{PW}$, and $c_{PP} = c_{WP}$. These conditions guarantee that if the capital/W-labor and capital/P-labor ratios are the same with K_W and K_P, respectively, the expected marginal products and utilities of both W-labor (and also P-labor) will be equal on W-capital and on P-capital. The equilibrium condition that $E_{WW}(u) = E_{PW}(u)$ requires, of course, that some W are working for P, as well as W, capital. Despite the necessity of the stringent assumptions to show that the number of W working for W-capital is exactly proportional to K_W, the result that most workers will be working for W-capital, if most capital is owned by W, will be quite robust.

with l_{PW}), by choosing loyalty to the W and no loyalty to the poor. In mathematical terms, this means choosing l_{WW} equal to unity, l_{PW} equal to zero.

Since most nonresidential capital is either owned or controlled by the wealthy, it may be assumed that K_W is large relative to K_P and hence it pays most W to train their children to be loyal to the W and not to the P.

C. Loyalties of the poor

The previous model agrees with empirical findings regarding the loyalties of the wealthy as described by Coles. How does it fare with respect to its predictions regarding the loyalties of the poor?

Insofar as the assumptions of the stringent model hold, it predicts that the poor will also be loyal to the wealthy in proportion $K_W/(K_P + K_W)$. This is consistent with Coles' findings regarding the teaching of poor mothers to their children, although this loyalty may be instilled more out of passive acceptance of the system than out of genuine enthusiasm – as suggested by the words of one very poor migrant mother: "Do you have a choice but to accept? ... Once, when I was little I seem to recall asking my uncle if there wasn't something you could do, but he said no, there wasn't and hush up. Now, I have to tell my kids the same, that you don't go around complaining – you just don't" (Coles, 1967, p. 52).

Of course there are cases that run counter to the predictions of the model, where the poor have not been loyal to those who provide them with jobs. The model, in fact, gives predictions where such conditions are likely to occur because its assumptions are violated. Where willing cooperation is not necessary from workers, it is not necessary to secure their active loyalty. Such devices as the assembly line force workers to work at the pace of the line irrespective of their mental attitude. Also, such incentive schemes as piecework, where the worker who puts in less effort receives correspondingly less pay, reduce the cost to the employer of unwilling workers, and therefore cause there to be less reason why firms should demand positive loyalty. In contrast, servants' cooperative willingness is often of positive value; and, correspondingly, the term "loyal servant" is a standard figure of speech.

Furthermore, social institutions may change the loyalty incentive structure. As one example, unions that interpose themselves between workers and the firm regarding work conditions reduce the positive incentives for workers to be cooperative. Welfare is another agency that reduces the incentives for parents to teach their children traditions of cooperation with employers, either rich or poor.

While this model is all too simple to predict class loyalties in many complicated situations, particularly where feelings of justice and fairness play an important role, nevertheless, in capturing some of the economic incentives for being cooperative (vs. noncooperative), this model does allow some comparative static analysis of class loyalties. At the minimum it serves as a reminder that an important side effect of social policy (toward unions and welfare, for example) is the resultant change in loyalties due to the change in incentive structure.

III. Institutional loyalties

The preceding sections have shown that parents eager to maximize their children's economic welfare may find it advantageous to teach honesty (Section I) and class loyalties (Section II) even though these traits may in some circumstances cause the individual to engage in nonmaximizing behavior. It pays parents to teach honesty and class loyalty because the *appearance* of honesty and class loyalty are beneficial; the easiest way to achieve these appearances is to *be* honest and loyal, even though honesty and loyalty themselves involve sacrifices.

This section presents a similar model of elite institutions. According to this model patriotism is jointly taught (i.e., jointly produced) with cultural values that are favorable to fellow graduates of the institution. This jointness of loyalties is reflected in the statement of President Eisenhower's defense secretary: "For years I have thought what was good for our country was good for General Motors and vice versa" (*New York Times,* 1954); likewise it is reflected in the college song which ends "for God, for country, and for Yale."

According to my model, loyalty to the institution has the effect that the services of graduates of the institution are highly valued – indeed, overvalued – by other graduates. Thus, while graduates of the institution may be patriotic even to the point of considerable self-sacrifice, the teaching of this patriotism may be of economic benefit to the graduates because it occurs jointly with the teaching of cultural biases in favor of the institution's graduates.

A. Examples

It may be helpful to give some concrete examples of institutions that, at least arguably, correspond to the model. In the United States, the military service academies teach loyalty to the academies themselves and also to the country. In Britain, Oxford and Cambridge – and, for some graduates, the public schools prior to university – teach loyalty to British values in general, and good government in particular. In addition, there appears to be considerable loyalty to fellow graduates. As one indication of this loyalty, most MPs of both the Labour and Conservative parties are graduates of these two universities; more remarkable still, eighteen out of twenty-two of Mrs. Thatcher's current cabinet members are graduates of public schools, and only two are nongraduates of Oxbridge or the Army-Navy service academies.

B. The model

In this model, it is assumed that the public has a choice (as in fact may not actually occur) between government by elite-school graduates and nongraduates. It is assumed that the nongraduates are loyal to themselves (because they have not been taught the elite patriotism), while the elitists are patriotic but with elite biases. The public, interested in good government, chooses the elite-school graduates as ministers. These graduates are patriotic and self-sacrificing, but in such a way that the interests of graduates are served on the average.

Assume that there are two types of persons – graduates and nongraduates. The government needs ministers in number equal to a fraction α of all graduates. These ministers, like other graduates, have a marginal product w outside the government. Graduates, being patriotic, are willing to serve as ministers for remuneration which is a fraction β of w. Ministers award government contracts. Ministers who are graduates value the services of other graduates at $(1 + \gamma)w$, whereas these services elsewhere only have value w. The fraction $(1 - \alpha)$ of graduates who do not work as ministers are hired by the government as long as their wage paid there exceeds their marginal products elsewhere. β and γ are both functions of the curriculum, denoted c, of the elite institution.

Nongraduates have no cultural biases, but, by assumption, they do not have the patriotism of the elite. Consequently, they wish to award government contracts for their own benefit; by assumption, it is impossible to check on such misappropriation, and therefore the return to the public from nongraduates is zero. The expected return from government contracts awarded by graduates to a graduate is w at a cost $(1 + \gamma)w$. Since the benefit–cost ratio of a government of graduates, even if not optimal, is higher than of nongraduates, the public chooses the former type of government.

Now consider the expected return to graduates which, if the economic-maximizing curriculum c is chosen, will be

$$(6) \quad \max_c \{\alpha\beta(c)w + (1 - \alpha)(1 + \gamma(c))w\}.$$

In the case of an internal equilibrium where curriculum is a continuous variable, the curriculum which is the economic optimum for graduates will meet the condition that the marginal decrease in wages due to self-sacrifice just balances the marginal return to other graduates, due to the overvaluing of their services. Note that the economic optimum for graduates in this model is not the economic optimum for the public. For the public, the best curriculum is one that *maximizes* the benefits net of costs of contracts, including the costs of hiring fellow graduates.

C. Summary

The following phenomenon has been modeled. Graduates of elitist institutions are often excellent at their jobs and genuinely interested in the "common welfare" as they see it. While they give less than the best possible service because of that elitism per se, however, that is better yet than what would be given by persons who remain untrained in values of patriotism and loyalty to the organization. The graduates on the average, although they sometimes do genuinely sacrificial service, still have a positive economic return, because what is lost due to their sacrifice is more than offset by the overvalue by the government in the award of government contracts. The net result yields less than the optimum to the nongraduate public; control of the elite curriculum, or other government regulations such as "affirmative action" hiring of nongraduates, will improve government benefit-cost performance.

IV. Conclusion

This paper has presented examples of the concept of loyalty filters and their potential importance for economic theory. According to the key idea underlying this paper, as persons go through different experiences, their loyalties change. Loyalty filters have implications for how individuals and institutions will attempt to reach specified goals, as illustrated above, where, in each of the three examples, the goal was the maximization of economic welfare. Loyalty filters, as well, have implications concerning the goals that individuals attempt to attain. The modeling of each of these aspects of reality constitutes a departure of importance from standard economic models, capable of explaining such phenomena as cooperative behavior, class loyalties, and much institutional behavior.

References

Akerlof, George A., "Labor Contracts as Partial Gift Exchange," *Quarterly Journal of Economics,* November 1982, *2.*

and Dickens, William T., "The Economic Consequences of Cognitive Dissonance," *American Economic Review,* June 1982, *72,* 307–19.

Allport, Gordon W., *The Nature of Prejudice,* Anchor Books ed., Garden City: Doubleday and Company, Inc., 1958.

Arnstein, Fred and Feigenbaum, Kenneth D., "Relationship of Three Motives to Choice in Prisoner's Dilemma," *Psychological Reports,* June 1967, *20,* 751–55.

Coles, Robert, *Migrants, Sharecroppers, Mountaineers,* Vol. II – *Children of Crisis,* Boston: Little, Brown and Company, 1967.

Privileged Ones: The Well-Off and the Rich in America, Vol. V – *Children of Crisis,* Boston: Little, Brown and Company, 1977.

Giddens, Anthony, *The Class Structure of the Advanced Societies,* New York: Harper and Row, 1975.

Gleitman, Henry, *Psychology,* New York: W. W. Norton, 1981.

Hirschman, Albert O., *Exit, Voice, and Loyalty.* Cambridge: Harvard University Press, 1970.

Homans, George C., *The Human Group,* New York: Harcourt, Brace & World, 1950.

Merton, Robert K., *Social Theory and Social Structure,* New York: The Free Press, 1956.

Sen, Amartya K., "Rational Fools: A Critique of the Behavioral Foundations of Economic Theory," *Philosophy and Public Affairs,* Summer 1977, *6,* 317–44.

Weber, Max, *The Protestant Ethic and The Spirit of Capitalism,* New York: Scribner's, 1958.

New York Times, Section VI, 4:4, February 28, 1954.

Index